THE *Legendary* UNDERGROUND RIVER OF GOLD

The Search Continues

GLENN A. TERRIS
EDITED BY JAMES TERRIS

outskirtspress
DENVER, COLORADO

The Legendary Underground River Of Gold
The Search Continues
All Rights Reserved.
Copyright © 2012 Glenn A. Terris
v4.0

Outskirts Press, Inc.
http://www.outskirtspress.com

ISBN: 978-1-4327-4803-6

Library of Congress Control Number: 2012914621

Outskirts Press and the "OP" logo are trademarks belonging to Outskirts Press, Inc.

PRINTED IN THE UNITED STATES OF AMERICA

Author and Wife Linda

Mildred and Ira Terris
Our Parents

WHEN IT SEEMS WE ARE LOST IN A FOG OF
CONFLICTING SIGNALS
WE CAN SEE YOU HOLDING A BEACON TO GUIDE OUR WAY

Contents

**SOME PEOPLE READ ABOUT HISTORY
OTHERS BECOME PART OF IT**

WHAT YOU ARE about to read is the ongoing search to prove or disprove the following sworn statement made by the now legendary Earl P. Dorr Notarized on the 10th day of December, 1934, in Pasadena, California. If completely true, it would be the largest cavern in the world. It would provide all the water ever needed for Las Vegas. It would make it legal for an underground Las Vegas in California. It would affect the value of gold worldwide.

TO WHOM IT MAY CONCERN:

This is to certify that there is located in San Bernardino County, California, about two hundred and fifty miles from Los Angeles, a certain cave. Traveling over state highways by automobile, the cave is reached in about ten hours.

A Civil Engineer. Mr. Morton, and I spent four days exploring the cave for more than eight miles. We carried with us Altimeters, Pedometers and a Theodolit, with which to observe and record actual directions, take elevations and measurements by triangulation.

Our exploration revealed the following facts:

1. From the mouth of the cave we descended as shown by the Altimeters to about 2000 feet, where we encountered a canyon, which from the Altimeters and by calculations we found to be from 3000 to 3500 feet deeper; making a total depth of 5400 feet from the mouth where we entered the caves to the floor of the canyon.

2. We found the cave divided into many caverns or chambers, of various sizes, all filled and embellished with Stalactites and Stalagmites, besides many grotesque and fantastic shapes that make these caves one of the wonders of the world.

3. The largest chamber we explored is about 300 ft. wide, 400 feet long and from 50 to 110 feet high. It is encrustated with crystals, fashioned into festoons of innumerable Stalactites, that hang from the ceiling, some of which are extremely large. One, the largest seen, is 27 feet in diameter and hangs 1,510 feet down into a 3000 ft. canyon. This great Stalactite is perpetually washed by water flowing down over it and falling into the dark canyon depths. The huge glistening white crystal is 500 feet longer than the Eifel Tower, and challenged us with amazement and wonder.

4. There is a flowing river on the floor of the canyon, which rises and falls with tidal regularity. All measurements and estimates of the river, including its tides and beach sands were reckoned by triangulation, taken with the Theodolit, and while we did not reach the

river, nevertheless, taking observations with our Theodolit and its telescope, we reckoned the river to be about 300 feet wide at high tide and 10 feet wide at low tide. It rises and falls from $7\frac{1}{2}$ to 8 feet. The Peysert brothers confirm our reckoning.

5. When the tide is out, there is exposed on both sides of the river from 100 to 150 feet of black sand, which the Peysert brothers report is very rich in placer gold. They report the sands on the river shore to be from 4 to 11 feet deep, and on an average about 8 feet deep.

6. There are numerous ledges above the canyon that are from 10 to 40 feet wide and covered with sand. We personally explored the ledge sands for a distance of more than eight miles, finding little variation in the depth and width of these ledge sands. And wherever examined, the ledge sands are found to be fabously rich in placer gold.

7. I have known intimately Oliver, Buck and George Peysert from my boyhood. I have discussed these caves with them repeatedly and thoroughly. They have reported to me in detail, their experience in exploring the caves. One of them, George, lost his life in the cave. Buck and Oliver say George was killed by diving in the river on the floor of the canyon. He struck an unseen rock, which killed him instantly. They have reported to me repeatedly their mining experiences and say they mined on the beach sands of the river a total in all of six weeks. They carried lumber down to the river and constructed a sluice box and, using a pump, the three mined for six weeks, during which time they recovered more than $57,000 in gold, (gold at $20.00 per ounce); they sent their gold directly to the U. S. Mint and banked the returns in a bank in Needles, California, and another bank in Las Vegas, Nevada. I last talked to them in my home about November 10th, 1934, at which time they repeated their former statements, giving information as to how they discovered the river; and more of their experiences in mining. They recovered several of the largest nuggets of gold ever found in California.

Both Mr. Morton and myself filled our pockets with the sands from the ledges, carried it out and had it assayed. Just what Mr. Morton's sand assayed, I do not know, but it was approximately $2,000 per ton.

- 2 -

I carried out ten pounds and two ounces of the ledge sand, and panned seven pounds, recovering more than $7.00 in gold, with gold at $20.00 an ounce. I sold the gold for $18.00 per ounce. The balance of my ten pounds of sand I sent to John Herman, a Los Angeles Assayer. His assay certificate shows a value of $2,144.47 per yard gold at $20.67 per ounce.

I, E. P. DORR, residing at 390 Adena Street, Pasadena, California, make the foregoing statements for the purpose of inducing investors to invest in the work of mining the gold in these caves, and I solemnly swear that all statements made hereinabove are true and that all persons will find the physical conditions in the cave as above stated.

C. P. Dorr

SUBSCRIBED and sworn to on this
10th day of December, 1934.

H. Hartwell Miller

Notary Public in and for the
County of Los Angeles, State of
California.

My Commission Expires Aug. 26, 1935

The Author (left), Tim (top right), and John (bottom right), Having
Breakfast on Death Valley Road to Ghost Town of Schwab 15 Minutes
Before the Flash Flood. This Spot Would Soon be Under Water.

CHAPTER 1

NINETEEN SEVENTY TWO was the year that I accidentally became part of the Legend of the Underground River of Gold. Though my profession was general manager of a national plastic manufacturer, my heart was of the California desert. Being a native of the state of Vermont, I was looking for a way to escape Southern California. The desert was the only solution I could find. For three years I made trips to the desert twice per month. Usually to Death Valley and the surrounding area. I started traveling alone. But, it soon was with friends and then led to business associates. My favorite trip would include at least two who had never been anywhere near a desert in their life.

One of those trips began in 1973 with a friend and two business associates. My friend had never been in the desert but lived in Southern California. My business associates were from Michigan and New York. The closest they had ever been to a desert was in an airplane flying over it.

On an October Friday evening I was preparing my supplies and vehicle as I waited for their arrival around midnight. I wanted to be well into the vast wilderness of the desert as the sun began to rise above the horizon. This is the only way to begin a visit to the true desert. By one AM all had arrived and following a check of all supplies it was time to leave the town of Diamond Bar where I lived at that time. I led the way with my Jeep Wrangler as they followed with another Jeep pulling a trailer. We would be in Baker, California, by 3:30 AM where we would leave Freeway I 15. This would be our last contact with the real world for a while so we took time to eat and top off both vehicles and cans with fuel.

From Baker we turned onto State Route 127 and traveled 58 miles to Shoshone. No sign of life in Shoshone. Perfect. From here we turned onto Route 178, the main road to Death Valley from the south. After nine miles we turned onto an unmarked dirt road near Ashford Mill that would take us into Green Valley. We were now in the desert.

After five miles we turned onto a very rough road that would lead to an impressive display of Indian Petroglyphs. The sun was showing signs of the first rays of a new day. Time to stay put, lower the tailgate, pull out the beer, (yes, I said beer) and celebrate as we watched the sun rise over the distant horizon. The visual beauty as the desert sand turned from black to purple to pink to light tan was breathtaking. The cacti could now be seen as they stretched their arms as if reaching for the sun.

By the third beer, we realized that we were not alone. The desert was full of life. A rabbit slowly hopped by. A rattlesnake could be seen moving to sun itself upon a rock. A mother quail followed by a parade of nearly twenty chics following in single file.

After an hour's studying the many Indian paintings, we returned to Green Valley Road and continued through an amazing valley for 20 miles until we reached a paved road that led us 5 miles to Dante's View. Our second beer stop. Dante's View is one not to miss. From an elevation of five thousand five hundred feet you look nearly straight down onto Bad Water, the lowest spot in the United States at two hundred eighty two feet below sea level. Looking across the Death Valley floor salt fields, you will see Telescope Peak rising nearly eleven thousand feet, the highest point in the Panamint Mountain Range. After a couple of beers, it was time to head for our next stop, the ghost town of Schwab, a distance of about twenty-five miles, to reach the dirt road near Furnace Creek Ranch. About 10 miles from Dante's View, off to the east against a mountain range, the buildings of New Ryan can be seen. This is the location of an old borax mine. A friendly caretaker still lived there in the 1970's.

We soon found ourselves at the turnoff point from route 190 onto another unmarked road to Schawb. This would be a remarkable 10 mile ride through a narrow canyon that opens into the bottom of a cereal bowl shaped dead end valley completely surrounded by mountains. By the time you reach the several buildings remaining of Schwab perched on one side of the valley, the entrance that you used has disappeared.

The story behind the town of Schwab is interesting in itself. The town was named in honor of Charles M. Schwab, president of Bethlehem Steel Corporation and a heavy investor in Rhyolite mines. The camp of Schwab in the midst of Echo Canyon was owned and promoted entirely by three women. Miss Fesler, a "blue-eyed blond with pretty teeth and a charming smile" and two married women "who were eager to colonize and increase the population." They formed the Schwab Townsite Company in January, 1907, and issued 30,000 shares at a dollar each. Men were reportedly eager purchasers. By March the camp had 200 people, including the usual floaters, and boasted a post office, a store, a restaurant, a very busy brothel, and a daily stage to Rhyolite. Before a newspaper and telephone could be brought into the camp, the district folded that same summer. Truth be known, the area was salted with gold, funded by Schwab, to sell the claims and set the girls up in business. There was never any gold in the area of the town of Schwab. There are buildings and foundations still that mark the site.

As we drove onto the Schwab road I pulled over to give instructions. "Follow me, be patient, call on the CB if you have a problem. There will be no roads to turn onto and get lost. We are on the only one. The canyon walls will reach two hundred feet and the canyon will narrow to 10 feet at points."

I had been up this road likely 15 times and thought I had given ample instructions. I soon would run into something I had

THE LEGENDARY UNDERGROUND RIVER OF GOLD

never experienced before. Following instructions and radio check I turned onto the dirt road to Schwab with the second Jeep about thirty feet behind. I called them and suggested that they back off to fifty feet due to the dust in the fan caused when there is water flowing out of the canyon. There is no road in the fan but would appear about one mile ahead as we entered the narrow canyon.

The weather was beautiful. Nothing but sunshine and not a cloud in the sky. But I soon noticed something strange. It looked as if small streams of water were starting to form near the top of the distant ledges. I knew that straight ahead, now about ¼ mile, was the entrance to the canyon. Within the canyon at about fifty feet was a sharp dogleg to the left. I looked to the sky and saw not the slightest sign of a cloud anywhere.

That was soon to change. As I looked towards the canyon entrance I noticed a strange haze. I stopped. I looked to the sky. No clouds. I looked to the nearby cliffs and saw that the little streams had increased in size. I looked back towards the entrance to the canyon, the haze looked darker. I saw no water but knew this was not a good sign.

"John. This is Glenn. Do you copy?"

"I copy. What is it, time for another beer?"

"No. Turn your Jeep around. NOW," I yelled into the microphone. "Don't even ask a question. Turn around. Don't wait for me. Head for the paved road as fast as you can or I will run over you," I demanded.

Unbelievably, by the time I turned around the water had reached me.

"If water hasn't reached you yet, it will soon," I warned them now ahead of me. "Do not respond. Just keep going as fast as you can. When the water reaches you you will not be able to see the gullies. You will have to follow the flow of the water. It will tell you where to go" I instructed as best I could.

By now the water was starting to push my Jeep. There was still no rain or clouds in the sky. "Where the Hell is the water coming from" I said to myself out loud. Tim, who was with me, sat in silence watching the water rushing by us and getting deeper. Suddenly the rain started. I could not see the other Jeep that was ahead of me. I was too busy to call, holding my vehicle where I wanted it to go. The water was now over bumper high and flowing by so fast there was a void in front of my Jeep that prevented flooding out my engine. I just had to read the water flow and hope I missed the ruts and gullies and boulders that were all around. If I was unsuccessful, we would likely drown.

It soon was as if the Jeep was floating. I am not certain it wasn't. But, we were going the right direction and turning the steering wheel seemed to have some positive effect.

"We are on the road," I could hear coming over the radio. "I can't see you. But, I can hear you coming," I heard.

By now I knew I was floating. But that changed as I hit something with my left wheel. I felt a gradual rise. The water was trying to turn me away to the right. I turned the wheel as hard as I could to the left and put my foot to the floor. I could see nothing now. Just hoped it was the right choice. Suddenly the front of the Jeep became fixed and the water continued to try now to pull the rear to the right. I floored the Jeep again and luckily the front wheel drive pulled out of the water and onto the paved road.

Still raining like Hell, but, I could see the other Jeep about thirty feet down the paved road from me. I drove to them and stopped, and shut down the engine. Tim and I sat in silence. Looking at each other shaking our heads. We both knew how close we came to possible death. We grabbed each other's arm in thanks and got out and stood next to the Jeep.

"You did a good job getting us out of there, Glenn," John said in thanks as he walked up to where we stood.

"I didn't plan that one," was all I could say.

It amazed me. I had never caught myself in a flash flood. I was always aware of the weather and possibilities of changes. There was no warning of bad weather in the area. I had listened to the last report on the national park station. No warnings were given. If we were in that canyon, which we would have been, within 3 to 5 minutes, we all would have died under water, against a wall, in our vehicles. The others did not really realize how close we came. They had never seen the inside of that canyon. But, it is narrow, the walls high, and full of sharp turns. Suddenly I felt my feet getting wet. I looked down and saw that the water was about to start running over the road.

"Come on. We must get out of here," I announced. "We are about 5 miles from the Ranger Station at the settlement of Death Valley. The road stays above the floor enough so we should be O.K."

I got into my Jeep with Tim. John and Bob followed in the other. It had begun to rain harder making it difficult to see the road, but I had been on it many times. We reached the parking lot across the road from the Ranger Station. We had been in water several inches deep but the parking lot was above water level so I turned into it. The entrance to the Ranger Station was closed and no one was in sight. Within about an hour the rain began to let up and we could actually see some breaks in the clouds. Looking across the highway I could see a couple of park rangers coming out of the building and head towards their trucks.

"I will be right back," I told the guys and headed across the highway to meet one of the trucks as it was leaving.

"How can I help you?" the ranger asked as I approached his truck.

"Are you expecting any more of this?"

"There are still storm cells in the area so it is very hard to tell," he replied. "I would not leave the highway. The park roads are all closed until we can determine the extent of the damage," he further instructed.

"O.K., sir," I acknowledged. "Thank you." As they left the Ranger Station and continued down the road, I crossed over to where I had left my friends.

"What did they have to say?" Bob asked.

"Not all that good. The park roads are closed," I replied. "We will have to leave the park or wait here until word the park roads are open. That could take days and even if they open them sooner they could be impassable."

"Where is the Wild Turkey?" I inquired. "Let's have a drink and decide what we want to do."

"I do have one idea," I announced as I took a sip. "I do know of a lot of places outside of the park. But I do not know how widespread this storm is. I do know of a place at Mountain Pass that sounds very interesting. It would be back to Highway 15 and then about 35 miles towards Las Vegas," I suggested. "We have to go back to the highway anyway so it is only a couple of hours out of the way. If it is nothing there are other places we can go on the way back. One thing is for sure. It is at a high altitude," I assured them.

"You have not been there?" John inquired.

"No. But I have been told of it by my sales manager and it sounds very interesting," I informed him. "It is a network of underground caverns that a group is exploring."

"Sounds good to me," John responded. "We certainly do not want to go back home now."

"Well. Let's get going," I said as I finished my drink and headed for the Jeep. "We have four hours of daylight left. That should give us time to get there before dark."

The devastation that resulted was astonishing. Even the highway was covered with mud and boulders that we had to weave around. As we reached the road that led to Schwab that we were on when the storm hit, the entire area was still completely under water. Several cars and trucks were stuck in mud and even one road grader.

The shortest route, 178, was closed so we had to take route 190 to Death Valley Junction, then Route 127 through Shoshone to Highway 15. We made it to a point eight miles south of Shoshone until just south of a road that went to the ghost town of Tecopa. Here we ran into a roadblock where the river was still flowing across the road. A state policeman told us that there was no way to go further. All roads were closed until morning. The policeman told us that we would have to park there for the night. There was a flat clear area where we could set up camp and that he would wake us when the road opened.

It was nearing dark. We parked and joined a few more people and camped for the night. It was really very quiet and beautiful lying on a lawn chair in a sleeping bag looking up at the moon as the fast moving clouds passed by on their journey accompanied by continuous flashes of lightning in the distance. We had now been up for 36 hours. After a couple more Wild Turkeys we were soon asleep.

CHAPTER 2

IT WAS STILL dark when we were suddenly awakened by the policeman. "There is another storm approaching and we must leave now and return to Shoshone," he yelled at us over the sound of the wind that was blowing nearly a steady 40 to 45 miles per hour and the nearly constant claps of thunder. "Hurry. We must leave now. Follow me."

We immediately threw everything into the Jeeps and headed with the other people north to Shoshone, a distance of about 8 miles. The rain had now hit and was coming down in sheets blown by wind gusts now reaching at least 60 miles per hour and likely higher. Lightning was continuous and actually hit the road twice between our vehicles.

The policeman pulled into a parking lot that went with some business but we could not see anything well enough to know what. He approached my vehicle and I opened my window. "You all stay here until at least morning, even if it stops raining. I must go back and set up road blocks at areas that do flood. Please stay until it is light and only leave if it has stopped raining," he told us. We all thanked him very much for he went way beyond what he had to do to make certain that we would be safe.

By 5 AM the rain had lightened up. It was still raining slightly but we could now get out of our vehicles and talk and enjoy a cigarette and warm up some coffee and brandy for breakfast. I tried to apologize to the guys for the interruptions and changes in the trip. But, they would not accept any. They all agreed that this was an experience way over and above what they had expected. I did have to agree. It had been exciting and fun despite how close we came to being caught in the canyon with death likely resulting. I do not believe any of them really realized how close that came to becoming a reality.

By 7 AM it looked safe to venture out. There was little lightning and only a light rain coming from broken clouds. We passed the place where we had parked earlier and could tell that it had flooded there but there was no running water now. We continued on to Baker, 48 miles south, for a real breakfast before continuing on Route 15 east 36 miles to Mountain Pass and the exit to the road to Kokoweef Mountain.

We would make one more stop before reaching Kokoweef. At the Cima road exit from Route 15, we would exit for a stop about two miles north of 15 to visit a little known WWII Japanese Internment Camp. It was used as housing and as a processing plant for copper that was mined in the nearby Clark Mountains. The largest mine was called the Standard. Many foundations remain and the most interesting are the several underground housings cut into the river banks used by the Japanese. These were small, about ten feet by ten feet and with a low ceiling. They were about five feet in height. One might still be able to enter them. A good sample of the deplorable conditions they lived in during the war. With shovel, easy samples of turquoise can be found. We spent about an hour here. Long enough for a couple of beers and then on to Mountain Pass and Kokoweef.

Once we reached Mountain Pass we took the Bailey Road exit and traveled the well maintained road about 7 miles. Kokoweef Peak stood proudly straight in front of us. At a fork in the road we took the right road and after a couple of sharp turns we could see the entrance to the mining camp. The first building we came to was on the left and looked like a small house and apparently the main meeting and cook house. Beyond that was a large pile of rock beside a small building with a sign that said cave rocks for sale. Further on the left was a large building that was used as

Kokoweef Mt. from west on Cima road (if you look closely you can see part of the road to the natural entrance on the left side of the mountain marked by an arrow).

a work shop. On the right side was a small trailer house and two small buildings used for housing. As soon as we entered the camp and exited our vehicles we noticed a large burly man with black hair heading our way from the main house.

"Greetings. My name is Marty. How may I help you?"

"My name is Glenn Terris. Your nephew Jerry works for me. When I told him that I was heading out this way he said that I should stop by because of my interest in this type of activity."

"Well," Marty replied. "Any friend of Jerry's is welcome here."

"He said that you are excavating and exploring some caverns," I inquired.

"Yes we are. Right up there," he answered as he pointed directly at the mountain in back of the house from which he had come.

"He also said that for a small fee you would give us a tour?"

"Hell. For free and we will put you to work," he responded.

"What do you say," I said as I looked at the guys who came with me. "Want to become miners?"

In unison they all replied, "Yes."

"Well. The crew is up there working now. They will be down soon for lunch," Marty explained. "I will talk to the boss, George, and see if you can join them for the afternoon. They will be blasting late today. They can use the help getting ready."

"If you plan to stay," he continued, "pull over to that building and make yourselves comfortable," Marty offered pointing to a small house between two Joshua trees.

"I must go in and get lunch ready for them. You are welcome to join us when they get here," he offered. "It will be soon."

As he entered the house he had come from we started to show our excitement. This had turned out to be a real adventure for all of us. After a short discussion we decided that this sounded as good as anything we could think of for the two days we had left. So, we proceeded to unload the Jeeps and trailer and set up camp.

The house was about twelve feet by eighteen feet. It had a table with a mismatch of chairs and four cot size beds. Just what we would need. Outside was a fire pit where we put the chairs we brought with us already planning the evening. We soon could hear the sound of the camp trucks indicating that the crew was arriving.

Three old vehicles soon entered the camp from the same road we had come in on. After a short look in our direction the five of them turned and entered the building. Not really knowing what to do, we just remained by the fire pit. It was but a minute or two and Marty opened the door and waved for us to come. Marty introduced us to what was a very welcome greeting. There were two young boys, likely 20 or 22. After all these years, I do not remember their names. But, they were part of the crew and lived there at the camp.

He also introduced us to George, the boss of the camp; Pat, the housekeeper, a nice but strange person; the Baron; Larry and his brother Ralph. We joined them for a nice lunch as they started to explain what was going on there. They worked on a volunteer basis. They provided food and a place to stay for those who helped and had no other place to go. This explained why some we would meet, as time went on, were just a little different.

We were told of the Earl Dorr history and what they were doing at the present time as they continued the elusive search for the way to the river. We were told that the company was now called Legendary Kokoweef Caverns, Inc., and that George was boss of the camp and Vice President. The President was Peter Tripolis of Pasadena, California. We also found out that if we wanted, we could buy shares in the company and be welcomed back anytime if we liked what we were about to do.

We soon found ourselves in the back of one of the old camp trucks riding the short distance around to the opposite side of Kokoweef Peak and up about half way to the top and a level area where they parked the trucks. We all first stared into the distance at the amazing view. We must have been able to see nearly to Las Vegas 60 miles away. "Come on you guys," George's command brought us back to reality. "You will find helmets with lights and gloves by the mine entrance. You must always put them on before entering," he ordered.

As I was putting on my gear I turned and looked across the outside area and noticed the rail tracks leading to the edge from within the mine. That told me that they were filling an oar cart with rock and dumping it outside. I was getting excited. I had spent years around old mines looking for nice rocks and going inside closed mines to look around. But, never had I ever worked with a mine crew.

The four of us followed the mine crew for about 200 yards into the mountain along the rails. It was well lit inside and though not running at the time, I could see that air could be pumped in through large pipes along the tunnel ceiling and water through smaller ones. I was impressed. The tunnel continued on but we followed up a metal ladder into a tunnel that went from the ceiling and rose at 45 degrees to an upper level about five hundred feet above. There was a level area at that point. I looked over my head and saw a metal Jacob's Ladder continuing straight up into a passageway that continued as far as I could see. However, we had to follow them around a wooden trough that extended down into another, but much smaller, tunnel at a near 90 degrees straight down. Beside the trough was a narrow wooden ladder that followed the contour of the rock on which to climb down. Interesting.

We were instructed to stay at specific locations along this trough starting at the top. There was a rope on a pulley that we were told had a five gallon bucket on the end. When we were told, we were to hand over hand pull the bucket to the top person who would dump the rock into the 45 degree tunnel we had just climbed up. That rock would end up below to be put into an oar cart and taken outside to dump. We had to transfer the bucket from one trough to another because there were corners in the passageway below. Also very interesting.

We spent the rest of the day doing just that. The purpose was to haul rock that was blocking the passageway which led lower into the mountain hoping that it would lead somewhere. This passageway was called Schnard's Hole after someone who first located it. We did very well. By the end of the day more than 500 buckets traveled up that trough. But, we were not done. There was another tunnel at the top of the 45 degree tunnel that followed level in another direction. We were told that they had a dynamite blast ready to blow to end the day and that we had to take all the lights out of the tunnel on the way down.

Before that, however, they invited us to light the fuse. We were fifty feet from the 45 degree tunnel that they called the raise, had to unhook the extension cord and lights that ran from there and the length of the raise which was a five hundred foot climb down on a metal ladder, and run the two hundred yards to the outside before the lit fuse ignited the dynamite. Very exciting I thought. The four of us looked at each other as if to say, "What the Hell did we get ourselves into?"

All but George and the four of us left the mine and went outside. George had two of us stand in the raise to help pull the lights out when they heard "FIRE IN THE HOLE." Bob and I stayed with George to carry gear out and hand to the next person. There were 14 fuses. One to a hole all drilled in a spiral fashion and each one, one inch shorter than the next, starting from the center. This was to break the rock into smaller pieces and so the blasts could be counted to be sure all 14 sticks ignited.

What seemed to be in slow motion, George lit the fuses, one at a time, then yelled "RUN. FIRE IN THE HOLE." He only had to say it once and we were on the way for the outside carrying gear and pulling what seemed to be a mile of extension cords and lights with us. We did make it out. Just as the blasting started. A muffled boom followed by a concussion wave and dust. What a rush it was. What a first day as a miner it was. That night we were invited to join the Kokoweef crew around their nightly campfire. They were going to tell us the story behind the "Legend of the Underground River of Gold" and the reason why they are still there.

Not long after dark, we could see from our cabin that George, Ralph, and Marty had a full fire burning. "Looks like it is about time for us to join them at their campfire," I announced. "Let's go." We walked the short distance towards their flickering fire. It was a moonless night allowing it to show off the beauty of the heavenly stars above together with the darkness of the desert night. "Hello, boys," George greeted us as we neared close enough to allow the fire to reflect off our faces. "Come on and join us by the fire and we will tell you the story that keeps us here." As soon as we all found a place to sit, a folding chair, a rock, or the ground, we grabbed a beer and George proceeded with "The Legend of the

Underground River of Gold" and of Kokoweef Peak.

"The legend actually starts in the mid 1800's with a battle between Mexican Desperadoes and a tribe of Paiute Indians," George began. "But, I will start with a cowboy named Earl Dorr and his friend, an old Paiute Indian. They worked together on Earl's father's cattle ranch near Colorado Springs."

CHAPTER 3

IT WAS THE end of another day for Earl on the range. As the sun slowly lowered within the waiting arms of the distant mountains, the dance of the shadows began their graceful sweeping movements across the far and near vistas. Appearing to have arms, the shadows reached within the valley below, cascading over rocks and stretching down the sloping terrain, to cast its own reflection upon the waters of the river as it flowed through the valley bottom as if to follow the now setting sun.

On a near ridge, standing next to his most precious earthly possession, his trusted horse, the silhouette of a man could be seen against the darkening sky. The colors of the sunset could not be matched with that of any other he had witnessed, as they slowly turned the sky from blue to a rainbow of blues, purples, and pinks. Serene shades began to reflect from river waters and browning grasses of the late fall season in Colorado.

"Come on, Buddy," the cowboy said to his companion, "it is time for us to go. White Eagle will be waiting for us and the fire will be warm." With hat in hand, he patted the rump of the horse, then turned for a parting look towards the darkening mountains. "So the end of another day comes," he said to no one but himself as he turned his horse and, commanding a slow pace, headed down into the valley below and towards the flickering light of a distant fire on the far side of the river.

It had been another long summer for the cowboy named Earl Dorr and his Indian friend White Eagle. He couldn't help but wonder if there would be another as White Eagle was aging. He also, as any cowboy would, began to wonder if this life in the wilderness mending fences, delivering calves, and seeing not a living soul but his one friend eight months of the year, was really worth it any more. By the time he was done in the range the hard winter would soon be upon them.

Dorr had grown up working on his father's vast open range ranch covering nearly as far as the eye could see. He now was getting restless for something new. His Indian friend had been with his father ever since he had been born. He also knew there had developed a close relationship between his father and White Eagle. His friend, White Eagle, had promised to tell the story before the Spirits called for him and he knew that time must be within the near future.

By now he had reached the waters of the river disrupting his thoughts to guide his horse across to the far side. The river was not deep or large by Colorado standards, but the rocks were tricky and Dorr could not take any chances of injury to his only means of travel. The thoughts of another hard winter approaching were also becoming thoughts of despair. As he approached the far side of the river he could begin to see his Indian friend sitting next to a very welcome sight. The warmth of the campfire. Following a brief pause, to allow his horse to drink from the river as the water drifted slowly by, he gave a squeeze with his knees and they continued on in the direction of the flickering light.

Soon they neared the light of the fire. Dorr paused his horse and dismounted. As he leaned against his trusted friend, he removed his hat and turned in the direction of the rising moon. Dorr was fighting within himself to stay. But he knew he couldn't. He wanted to leave. But, where would he go? What would he do? Dorr slowly walked his horse past the fire. With a tip of his hat, as a gesture of hello, he continued past the fire and tied his horse up on horse run--a rope tied between two trees. After placing feed and water, the uncertain cowboy turned and walked to White Eagle sitting next to the warm fire.

"White Eagle," Dorr spoke as he approached, "I do not have any idea why, but, I have something or someone in my head telling me that this could be our last summer together. That it is time for us to move on. To move south before the snow arrives." White Eagle offered no response other than extending his arm with a gesture for him to sit with him by the fire.

"Coffee, my son," he offered handing his new arrival a cup.

"Thank you," he gracefully answered as he accepted the out-reached cup of coffee and sat on a rock across from his friend close to the fire.

Both sat in silence staring into the flickering glow and shadows created by the wavering flames before them. Visions of the past winters and past summers drifted through their minds. Neither anxious to be the one to begin the next sentence. As his mind briefly returned to the present, Dorr wondered why he was having these thoughts and what they would lead to. Finding no answer, his mind slowly drifted back into the depths of the campfire.

White Eagle, being a full blooded Paiute Indian, was long on years, but also long on knowledge. Having spent most of his years with the white man, other than the evidence of skin color and facial features, to talk with him was as talking to another white man. With White Eagle's long association with the white fellowship, his language had lost most of its reflections of his natural Paiute. However, this did not have any telling indication of influence in regard to his beliefs, knowledge, or spiritual intuitiveness.

As Dorr again returned mentally to the present, he rose from the rock he was sitting on and walked the short distance to his horse. Reaching into his saddle bag, he recovered a bottle of whiskey. Slowly turning he returned to his place on the rock he had been sitting. With a glance towards the non-responding White Eagle, he took a large swallow of the whiskey and then returned to his thoughts as he again stared into the fire. Following a long pause, he raised his head. Turning his eyes into the direction of

White Eagle, Dorr was surprised to find him looking back at him.

"What is it that you want to say?" Dorr finally inquired following what seemed to be an eternal stare.

"You leave soon," White Eagle responded quietly. "You get your pay and leave with the next sun. I am old and tired. Too old to travel as far as the Spirits are calling for you to go. I know where the Spirits say you should be. You must do as they say," he continued.

With another swallow from his bottle of whiskey, Dorr lowered his head and returned to a stare into the depths of the fire. It was a surprise that White Eagle seemed to know what he had been contemplating throughout the day. Was it the same Spirits that were placing these thoughts into his head that White Eagle was talking about? It appeared as though that must be true.

"I have also been thinking that I would soon be leaving," Dorr said as he raised his eyes to meet White Eagle once again. "But, I can't leave to go anywhere unless you go with me," he continued with a strain in his voice.

"It is time for you to go. But I must stay. It is my time to rest in waiting for my sign to be with the Spirits," White Eagle insisted. "The Spirits tell me that I must share with you what I know. They say for me to tell you, my trusted friend, their message. You listen to what I have to tell you. Then sleep. You must get your money you have earned, then leave to your new calling. The Spirits have chosen you. You must not defy them," White Eagle explained with emphasis.

As the old Indian sat in silence, Dorr stood with his bottle, turned, and walked the short distance into the near darkness, where his horse stood. He needed to share his thoughts with someone. Who would be better than his horse? Soon Dorr returned to the rock by the fire, sat down and looked once again at White Eagle.

"What is it you have that is to be told?" he questioned.

"There is a mountain far from here," he began his story. "Deep under this mountain is a river. A river which runs through big rooms with sands of gold."

Dorr, having a greedy aspect within him, took a long swallow from his bottle and gave White Eagle a long and piercing look of doubt.

"Is this one of those bullshit Indian stories," he thought suspiciously as he reached his hands towards the warmth of the campfire.

"The Spirits tell me to tell you, not of locoweed. The truth," White Eagle responded sharply showing his Indian temperament.

"I have seen what I tell you. I have been to the water below a vast dry land that I have told you about. I have felt the coldness of the water. I have held the golden sand from its banks. Yellow sand from the rocks above the river," his Indian friend insisted.

"If this is true, what the Hell are you doing here?" the unbelieving Dorr exclaimed.

"My brothers and I went to the shores of this sacred river many times to bring back the sand for our people. We would trade with our Shoshoni brothers for charcoal they make from Pinyon Pine trees that grow in the high mountains where they live," White Eagle continued. "The last time to the river, one of my brothers fell into the darkness below. We could never find him and his spirit remains in the waters of the river. His spirit still cries. No Paiutes can return to this place until his Spirit rests with the Gods. It is a place sacred to all Paiutes."

White Eagle did not reply further as this was a story that had not before been told, and he wanted this aspect to be left to Dorr's own interpretation of the facts as his mind searched for its own signs from the Spirits. White Eagle also was waiting for signs of his own from the Spirits for guidance as to how much and what he should tell Dorr. He believed that the Spirits would guide him as Dorr reacted to what he heard and learned from what he was told.

Dorr rose from the rock he was sitting on by the fire and walked into the near darkness once again as he tried to absorb what was the beginning of an astonishing story. But, how astonishing he was still to learn. He soon returned and confronted his story teller. "Tell me again, please. All that gold down there and no one knows about it?"

"Yes," was his immediate and forceful response. "That mountain was the home to my people for many, many, winters. My people had to sacrifice the river, the yellow sand, and the mountain, until our Gods told me to speak of it. That made life very hard for us because we lost what we traded. The Gods now say to tell you. It is not for me to question any word or sign. For it is to be, what the Gods say it is to be."

"Can you take me there and show me where it is?" Dorr questioned.

"No. I am of too many years to travel that many horizons. But, I can tell you the way," he promised.

"I must stop now and talk to the Spirits," White Eagle announced. "I must seek their guidance. When I return, I will tell you as they instruct me."

Dorr had nothing he could do at this point but wait as he watched White Eagle slowly raise his tired body. This cowboy watched him in wonderment as he stood and appeared to talk to the fire in a chant in natural Paiute. He had not seen this spiritual side of his friend often, and never before to this extent. He also had no idea what he was saying. His old partner then raised his head to the night sky and, with arms outstretched, spoke words directly to the Gods in the sky.

Without looking towards Dorr, White Eagle then turned from the fire, lowered his head and softly spoke as if to himself, as he looked to the ground. Soon the confused cowboy looked towards the trees in front of him and slowly walked into the darkness of the woods in silence. Following a few moments of looking at the spot from which White Eagle had disappeared, Dorr returned to his seat and reached for his bottle of whiskey. Unknown to him the story he would soon be told would be his entire life forever. Into a storied life that would not only affect the rest of his life, but would influence that of others for generations.

The remainder of the story would have to wait until White Eagle returned from his meeting with his Gods as he needed their guidance and signs of acceptance to continue. In the meantime, the excitement of the story together with the imagination of his thoughts, which was a very questionable combination, especially combined with his intake of whiskey, had to wait until at least morning if it was to be told at all.

CHAPTER 4

THE FIRST SIGNS of morning began to appear, as would soon the sun within the distant mountains that formed the horizon. A hint of morning chill was evident as the fire had returned to but a flicker of the life it once had. With much peacefulness and grace, the sky to the east turned from its night darkness as a soft salmon color became prominent. Movement could be noticed within the bedroll where Dorr had been sleeping. Still unknown to the awakening cowboy, was the figure of White Eagle sitting nearby on the far side of the fire looking in his direction. White Eagle reached for more wood and, with the grace in movement of the eagle for which he was named, placed it carefully on the dim fire. He watched without movement as Dorr began to rise from his sleeping place and turned away as he reached to help stir a little more life into the fire to warm the brisk morning air.

"It is time for me to tell you of my people as the Gods have instructed," White Eagle said finally breaking the silence as he startled the still half asleep range hand.

"You make coffee. Then I start to tell you," he further instructed.

Without a word, Dorr stoked the fire, added more wood and continued to make the much needed coffee as he was instructed. After pouring his coffee he proceeded to sit next to the fire in silence as he waited for White Eagle to speak. There was no way that the unsuspecting cowboy could have possibly known that the story he was to be told would become a legend of great proportion that, to this day, still mystifies anyone who would set foot on that mountain. A mountain now known as Kokoweef. A mountain that stands silently high above the nearby peaks, withholding many secrets from all but White Eagle and his brothers.

"At a time many, many seasons ago," White Eagle began his story of wonderment, "one of my people stood on a high rock looking out into the distant desert before him."

Dorr could immediately feel himself strangely being pulled to what he was listening to. It was if he were drifting from his spot by the fire to some distant place he had never been or seen. To look at him, it could be noticed that his stare was soon being replaced by closed eyes as his mind began to close out all previous thoughts and drift to another world. It was if White Eagle somehow had withdrawn all thoughts and hypnotized him, thus placing him into the story he was being told. This was a place much different from the land he was used to. Strange things could be seen growing. Not at all like the trees he was used to. He had heard of cactus but had never seen any such as these. Some standing as poles with arms. Some looking as woody bushes with leaves being replaced by long sharp needles. Many had flowers of a very radiant color. Whatever the color--red, yellow, or purple--they were very beautiful. Dorr listened intently as White Eagle continued.

As the Indian stood on the rock, high above the sprawling terrain below, the sun was just showing its influence. Shadows could now be noticed as the cacti began to make their presence known. Slowly the sands and rocks turned from gray to an artist's pallet of beiges, pinks, and browns, broken only occasionally by the green of a cactus or small clump of desert grass.

Scanning the horizon the Indian searched for movement with bow and arrow ready. He was watching for any deer, rabbit, snake, or other desert critter which would do for his family's meal for the day. Suddenly, with his trained eye focused on a clump of cacti, he could see a movement on the far hilltop. A shadow of something the size of a very large deer began to move from the protection the desert plant had given. What he saw did not look like any deer he had ever seen before. It appeared to have a growth protruding from its back. For what seemed an eternity, the Indian watched his curious subject as it slowly scaled the rocks and carefully made its way to the bottom of the hill and the location of a dry wash. By this time light was becoming more prominent and he could tell that this was no deer. It appeared to be something of half-man and half-animal.

By now Dorr began to realize that he was about to hear a long story. But, a story he wanted to hear every word of. He remained silent and motionless as the story unfolded into a tale that would consume the rest of his life and that of many to come after him.

Secretly, the Indian watched the rider as he hid behind a near-by Joshua tree. Despite the ever prevailing feeling of fear that was slowly overtaking him, the Indian's curiosity prevented him from retreating as the rider neared his place of hiding. With arrow ready, the inquisitive Indian watched motionless in a state of wonderment. Suddenly, the rider stopped. As he looked in the direction of the watching Indian, it became obvious that he had been spotted.

Following a short pause, the cowboy directed his horse and cautiously moved in the direction of the Indian. At what appeared to be a safe distance, the cowboy paused and motioned for him to come from his now known hiding place. Soon the Indian did as instructed and gradually appeared from his place behind the cactus and stood in silence staring at a sight he could not believe; a man on a strange looking deer. The rider proceeded to move his horse closer to the frightened Indian as he had not known of any hostile tribes in the area.

"I am Ramon. I look for water for my horse," he spoke as he broke the silence.

As the Indian continued to stand motionless in silence, the cowboy noticed a very large gold nugget which hung by twine around the Indian's neck. With a look of bewilderment, the native moved ever closer and pointed with a shaking hand at the strange animal under the bronze skinned man upon its back.

"This is a horse," the rider explained.

"It walk for you?" he further questioned.

"Yes. It also runs very fast," was his answer.

"Where did you get that which you have hanging around your neck?" the curious rider asked as he pointed to the necklace with the shining rock hanging upon his chest. Without a word the warrior turned and pointed in the direction of a far high mountain peak. He then followed by pointing toward the ground at his feet and then back towards the mountain.

"Do your people live there?" he asked. With but a nod of his head the Indian indicated that they did.

"I will give your people horses if you will show me," Ramon offered.

"You come to this place with the next sun," was his response. "Now you go."

With a nod in gesture, the rider turned his horse away and returned from where he had come through the wash and vanished within the Joshua on the far side of the rocky gully. Without hesitation and abandoning his search for water, he slapped his horse and returned to where the rest of his one hundred strong band of desperadoes had camped for the now approaching night. Directly he led his horse through camp to the surprise of all until he approached the tent of Orelio Rodrigues, their leader.

"Orelio," he excitedly exclaimed as he dismounted from his horse in haste, "You will not believe what I have found."

"Water, I hope," was his reply as the leader walked from his tent to where Ramon had stopped.

"No. An Indian," he answered showing excitement that only further irritated his leader.

With a look of displeasure Orelio turned and entered his tent with Ramon following close behind.

"Wait. He had a gold nugget around his neck as big as your eye," Ramon tried to defend himself desperately. "He said his people would show where it came from if we gave them some horses."

"Why would they do that just for a few worn out horses?" Orelio questioned suspiciously.

"He didn't even know what the Hell a horse was. Do you realize what it would mean to these Indians if they had horses and would not have to walk on foot for food and water in this Hellish land that they must exist in," Ramon pleaded his case. "Look at what we have crossed. They have to live in it."

"I guess that you are right," the now interested leader replied. "But, of course, we won't give them the horses once they tell us," he suggested as he reached for his bottle of tequila.

Ramon's facial expression quickly changed from a look of desperation and fear of repercussions for what he had done to a sheepish grin.

"Here. Have a drink," Orelio offered in good gesture as he handed Ramon the bottle.

Without hesitation, Ramon grabbed the bottle and with a thrust to his tilted head, downed as much as he could swallow. So the plan was set. Not knowing what the Indians had in mind, they at least knew what their own intentions were. They would go to near the location that Ramon was to meet the Indian. Let him go ahead with a few men and several horses as the rest of them held back to follow them from a distance. Ramon and his complement of men and horses would meet the unsuspecting Indian and, showing an outward appearance of friendship, follow him to his village.

All was soon to change as soon as they were told the secret of where the gold nugget had come from. They were destined to become slaves of the desperadoes and be at the ill-intentioned will of their captors. It was well known to the Mexicans that the Paiute Nation was of peaceful nature. Never had the unsuspecting Indians experienced what Hell they soon would face. Outsiders in this land were new to them. This had always been their land to live in unmolested. Untouched by those from a world they knew nothing about. To them gold was of no value other than to use for trade with the Shoshone Indians to the north for charcoal, nuts, and berries. Only now had people such as the Mexicans ventured north into the vast, dry, hostile desert.

CHAPTER 5

AS THE FIRST virgin rays of the morning sun began to appear on the desert sands, the ruthless band of Mexican renegades was already upon their horses and riding towards their rendezvous with the unsuspecting Paiute Indians. A peaceful tribe expecting nothing but a meeting of benefit to both parties. That benefit for both was to be their gold, of which they had a seemingly endless supply, for horses that would provide an expansion beyond anything they could have imagined, in this harsh land which they called home.

Gold to the Paiutes was but a thing of beauty. But also of survival. Gold they traded with the tribes to the north, such as the Shoshoni and the Washo, for charcoal, nuts, berries, and hides. This wonderful transaction that they had hoped for this day was not to come. If it had, as they believed their Spirits had delivered to them, it would have made those needed trades for supplies much more unconstrained. These possibilities, together with the fact that they had never faced or experienced hostile people in their known history, opened the door which led them to the danger and the circumstances which they unknowingly were about to encounter. It was not a reason of ignorance but of a fact of living an untouched and undisturbed life of peace in their land and with a life of their own. What they were about to face within their very near future would affect the Paiute Indians to this day.

The desert seemed ever so peaceful as the first morning sun rays began their dance across the desert sand. So deceiving that they were far from what reality was to bring to this forsaken land. Not a sound could be heard but those of the blowing winds stirred by the warmth of the now strengthening sun rays and that of a distant coyote as it called from the horizon. There is a Heaven within this land but a Hell awaits that can kill without warning if given the slightest opportunity. For the unsuspecting Paiutes, that Hell was soon to show its ugly head in the gravest of ways.

The rising dust of nearly a hundred Mexicans upon their horses could be seen in the distance as it rose to create a disturbing orange glow through the morning sunlight as they made their way towards the sleeping Indian village. Soon the Mexicans could be seen as they reached a high cleft overlooking the peaceful unsuspecting Indian village. Smoke slowly drifted into the morning sky, giving the appearance of what was to be another beautiful day in this unchanged land of rock and sand of every possible shade of brown, beige, purple, and pink. Of cactus, Joshua trees, and snakes.

"There it is," Ramon informed Orelio as they looked towards the village below. "I think that we should approach appearing as friends as they expect for a few days. Then we can make our move in surprise," Ramon suggested.

"I agree," Orelio responded. "That will give us a chance to get all the information of the gold and its location that we need."

"Sounds like a good idea," Ramon agreed as he motioned for the band to proceed on towards the village. As they approached the quiet village they found what could be called a welcoming party of friendly souls waiting to greet their soon-to-be worst enemy. An enemy that was destined to destroy them if it was necessary to feed their own greed and hunger for power.

Silver Hawk was the first to meet them as he stood several strides in front of the rest of the villagers as the Mexicans approached. Without a word spoken, Silver Hawk motioned for Ramon to follow then turned and walked towards his Indian brothers. As requested, Ramon lowered himself from his horse, grabbed the horse's rein, and followed him. Close behind the band of Mexicans followed.

Silver Hawk led them to a nearby tepee of obvious different status from the others. Without speaking, he motioned for them to stop, and entered the tepee with Ramon following. Nervously, the rest of the strangers waited for their greeter to return from the tepee into which he had disappeared, followed by Ramon. As the long moments slowly passed, the curious Indians closed in around the Mexican strangers as they stood fast on their never before seen horses.

Following what seemed an eternity, Silver Hawk, Ramon, and tribal chief, appeared as they exited the tepee and approached the Mexicans. Finally the chief walked to one of the strange look-ing animals and cautiously reached to touch it. As his hand first touched the animal, he quickly retracted it. But seeing no motion from what he had done, he reached toward the animal once again. This time a curious smile slowly appeared on his face. His smile appeared to be his sign of acceptance. With that, the rest of the tribe again approached closer to the animals. One by one reach-ing slowly to touch.

"We will now take you to the yellow stones," Silver Hawk sud-denly offered, thus eliminating the Mexicans' plan to show their untrue friendly intentions for a few days.

"Tell them that they may ride the horses we brought for them," Orelio offered.

"They will not, now," Sliver Hawk replied. "After they see you ride first. Then they might try," he explained.

"O.K., then let's go to where the yellow stones are," Ramon directed as he attempted to hide his true desire and intent.

"You follow," Silver Hawk instructed and turned to face the distant mountain peak. "I will now take you there."

A party of braves were chosen to lead the Mexicans. Only three Mexicans were allowed to follow.

CHAPTER 6

THE DISTANCE TO the mountain was but a short travel to the inexperienced eye. With the Indian village located on the edge of a large plateau, the mountain of destination located on the distant side had the appearance of being much closer than in reality it was. It would turn out to be nearly noon by the time they could reach the base of the mountain.

The mountain was steep but there was a switchback path that led up the side. Despite being but a climb of nearly one thousand feet to the cave entrance, the mountain's appearance was an awesome sight, enhanced by another one thousand feet to the summit. It displayed an angry aura about itself that could be felt without words, as if to be a warning from within. This mountain peak stood above the surrounding terrain as a symbol as a massive monument of hardness and bold strength. Standing alone surrounded by the Joshua covered valleys below, the mountain was covered with only rough, jagged rock outcroppings of lethal points and but very few areas of vegetation.

"There," Silver Hawk announced as he pointed to a point near the base of a cliff nearly half way to the top of the mountain, "that is where we will find the entrance to where yellow sand is, in a river far below. We must leave the animals here as it is much too steep for them from this point," Silver Hawk further instructed.

In a single line the Mexicans were led up the narrow, twist back trail. With each turn was a 180 degree turn resulting in a complete change in direction. Back and forth across the face of the mountain peak and gaining height with each turn they slowly reached a point at the base of a sheer rock ledge of about twenty feet in height. It had taken them another excruciating two hours to reach this point up the mountainside. What they found was of great surprise to all of the Mexican guests. Nothing was to be immediately seen but a small hole, about two feet in diameter and leading straight down into the black confines of the inner reaches of the mountain.

"This is the only way to where the yellow sand is?" Ramon exclaimed loudly with a sharp tone in his voice as he looked into the darkness below him just in front of his feet.

"There is another," the Indian informed him. "But, it is a burial ground for people. Another people from many, many, winters before. That is another, but forbidden way," was his only answer.

The Mexicans could but stand in silence as they looked at one another in questionable glances about what they had been told. They all had known very well of the stories told of the treasures which existed within these grounds left from a people long past from these times. There were many questions that they wanted to ask at this point, but, to avoid raising suspicion, none were raised but saved for another time.

"What is down there?" Ramon finally questioned as he broke the silence as they stood next to this black hole within the rocks.

"There is a river with sand of yellow color on both sides and on the bottom beneath the water," Silver Hawk answered.

"How far down in there is the river?" Ramon asked as he leaned down in an attempt to see into the darkness within the hole in the mountain.

"It takes two suns to reach the river."

"Straight down?" Ramon responded as he stepped back from his position near the opening.

"Yes. Through white rooms connected by narrow passes. Rooms white with which grows from the walls," Silver Hawk tried to describe.

"Big room, small rooms, all as beautiful as the Spirits' sunsets," he continued. "Long pointed rocks like the horns of a dear grow from the room top and bottom. All like a room of snow."

"There must be a lot of locoweed growing around here," Ramon said softly in disbelief as he turned to look into the vastness of the plateau below him.

During the days to follow, several attempts were made by the Mexicans to follow their Indian guides down within the blackness below, exposed by the small opening in the side of the mysterious mountain. From the very entrance it was a matter of descending straight down within the grips of the unknown below them. Adding to the mystery of the unknown was the obvious flow of cold air from within. It was soon becoming a popular feeling that the difficulty within this passage of shear descent was why the Indians were not hesitant to show them the way to the yellow sand hidden within the bowels of the mountain below. The Mexicans were not the sure footed Indians and soon found it necessary to return to the surface with each attempt.

With light, provided by roots soaked in creosote, the Indians could descend the near vertical walls without fear, leaving far behind the frustrated Mexicans. The Mexicans soon gave up their futile attempt to lower themselves into the mountain and settled on making camp and watching the Indians reappear from the cavern with their leather sacks filled with what was gold. More gold in a matter of days than they had seen in a lifetime.

Soon the Mexicans found themselves sitting by the fire again, alone with their bottles of drinking spirits. A few of the Indians had left to return to the village with the gold recovered as the remaining Indians had returned to within the mountain for more. "We must find the other entrance," Ramon commented as he and the others sat around the evening camp fire.

"But, how will we get them to show us where it is?" Francisco asked.

"I do not know," Ramon responded. "But, unless we do, we

may not get to the gold. Maybe we can get one of the Indians drunk. Not being used to what we have."

"We must stay friendly until we can figure out a way," Orelio added.

CHAPTER 7

FOR THE FOLLOWING several days the frustration mounted as they watched the Indians return from the mountain with sacks filled with gold from the depths of the caverns within. Temptation was rampant to just steal the gold recovered since they arrived but they were well aware of the fact that much would be lost if they did. It was finally decided that it was time to make a move and to somehow locate the other and sacred entrance, which would lead them to the riches below without the need of the Indians other than as captive slaves. With the benefit of their horses and high powered rifles, the decision was made to cover the vast territory around the village and return with enough deer for a feast these Indians could have only imagined. Their true intent was to secure the information to locate the entrance that would give them easy access to the caverns and gold below.

Ramon approached Silver Hawk with his plans of a feast, which he thought was a wonderful exhibition of appreciation to their new found friends. The Indians then were to wait for their brothers to return from the caverns which would take another day as the last party had been in the mountain since the morning before and not due until the following morning. The three Mexicans, together with a small party of the Indian braves, returned to the village.

Once they arrived at the village Ramon and Orelio headed straight to their camp just outside the village to make plans. Meanwhile the Indians that returned with them to the village had gathered their people and told them of the impending festive time that was being planned. From the Mexicans' camp all attention briefly was turned to the gleeful sounds that were coming from the

Indians celebrating.

"If they only knew what was going to happen they would not be dancing that dance," Ramon exclaimed to all that could hear with an obvious impudent tone.

"Let's go and find their last meal," Ramon commanded as he climbed upon his horse.

Immediately, all but a few to watch over camp hastened to their horses and followed Ramon out of camp and towards the open plateau to begin their hunt. For the following several hours the Mexicans divided into small bands and spread throughout the flatlands and near small hills. Occasional shots could be heard from their rifles indicating a successful hunt. The entire day was killing and preparing their game for the short trip back to the village. Once all was ready, the deer cleaned and placed on horses for the return, it was time for a short celebration of their own. They found a bottle and began their own dance of craziness until darkness was showing its first signs of approaching. Ramon finally climbed upon his horse and commanded the rest to follow. "Come on, that is enough fun, it is time to go. We have a long night ahead of us." The Mexicans then mounted their horses and turned them in the direction of the village and the beginning of what was to be a night of slaughter, rape, and Hell.

As the Mexicans entered the village they were pleased to find that most of the Indians were well on their way to drunkenness. Quickly the Mexicans were surrounded by the celebrating, yelling braves as they ran to greet them and gander at the deer on the pack horses. Without hesitation or silence of their yells, the Indians cut the ropes holding the deer. Some deer fell to the ground as others never made it past the shoulder of a waiting brave as he carried it to a near fire pit. As soon as the braves reached the fire pit area several began preparing the ones which were to become the centerpiece of the celebration.

By now the festivities had taken total control of the Indians as they were well on their way to total intoxication as the Mexicans had planned. Meanwhile the Indian braves continued to celebrate and, one by one, fell to the ground as they passed out. The squaws could be found in the bedrolls of most any of the Mexicans. Some appeared agreeable, but some were struggling to get away from their unwanted encounter.

It soon became obvious that it would be one of the squaws that would lead the Mexicans to the elusive easier entrance to the cavern system so that they could retrieve the gold themselves or enslave the Indians and stop this mendacious friendship. Well into the night the festivities continued until not a sober Indian could be found. This fact, combined with the ever growing impatience among the Mexicans, signaled that the time for them to make their move had come.

Suddenly Ramon grabbed the squaw who had been fondling him and stuck a knife to her throat. Without a word, the squaw pushed herself from Ramon, motioned "yes," and started walking away from camp in a direction that took them into the opposite direction from the mountain.

"It is this way," she half pleaded him to follow out of fear.

"If it is not in that direction, you shall never return," Ramon warned as he pushed her in the direction she indicated. For the next several hours Ramon and Francisco followed her across the valley and towards another distant small mountain.

"It is up there," she informed them as she pointed towards the side of the hill she had indicated.

"Then take us there," Ramon insisted. Once they reached a location high on the side of the hill, she pointed to a cave and told them that she could go no further.

"You go. I cannot. It is sacred ground."

The two Mexicans proceeded to tie her to a nearby cactus and left her as they headed for the newly discovered cave entrance. What they were about to find was to be far beyond anything they had imagined. Even their thoughts of the gold would be displaced for a time.

CHAPTER 8

WITH THE AID of a single willow bush burning and wrapped tightly for light, the Mexicans cautiously entered the dark confines of the cave to which they were led. Bending slightly, as the entrance was no more than three feet in height, they entered into a room soon to increase in size to more than ten feet wide by seven feet in height. How deep within the mountain the cave extended could not be seen.

"Do you see anything, yet?" Ramon questioned.

"I see nothing," his immediate response could be heard as Francisco answered from within the darkness ahead.

In silence, they continued further into the cave in search of the way to the River of Gold that they were told was awaiting them below within the sacred cave. Carefully, with the one light giving them their only guidance, they looked deep into every crack and crevice that became evident on the passing walls and ceiling. With each step they searched the floor in front of them the short distance they could see for any sign of change. For any hole or drop off.

Suddenly, Ramon stopped and looked back at Francisco as he held the burning stick higher above his head. With an expression of anxiety he turned and continued on, speaking not a word. They began to shiver. Was it the cold chill of the damp cave? Or, was it fear that they felt as they continued on into the darkness that prevailed in this world. A world into which they had entered with its feeling of confinement created by the walls of the passageway. At this point the outside light could not be seen as the hole into which they had gone was now deeper and deeper within the mountain.

It was a strange sight to behold. Cold, black, what appeared to be a white cloud drifted from within the cave ahead of them, as it reached for the warmer air of the outside. Creeping around them as if trying to consume all that dared to enter. The temperature within the cave was never affected by the outside temperature as it maintained a near constant 54 to 58 degrees. They felt as though they were being drawn into a cold Hell, never to return to the world from which they had come. Knowing full well that their torch would not last long added to their fear, for the long creosote dipped willow stick was not meant to last long.

When the Indians needed light for a long period of time, such as when they entered the caves, they would use a special torch. The torch would be made from the creosote bush but would be wrapped at the end with hemp that had been dipped in grease. This grease was made from buffalo hide scraped with elk horn scrapers. The fat was rendered into the grease. The Indians knew how long these torches would last but the Mexicans had no idea.

"Oh Hell," Ramon suddenly exclaimed breaking the deadly silence as he lurched back nearly knocking Francisco off his feet.

"What the Hell is wrong with you?" Francisco fearfully asked as he regained his balance.

"It's---it's---it's a body! There is a fucking body on that rock ledge there," Ramon answered as he lifted his torch towards the wall just in front of him.

Ramon stood stiffly in his spot. He could do nothing but stare in total disbelief at what appeared to be the body of an Indian carefully placed on a ledge in the cave. Francisco slowly moved ahead to where Ramon was standing and joined him as they stared together in surprise and fear. What they had found was the first of several mummified remains of an ancient people. With each they also found many items of fabulous value in the form of statues made of solid gold.

"What the Hell have we found? What the Hell kind of Indians

are these?" Ramon asked as he stood and stared at what they had discovered.

"They look to be what I have heard to be found in Mexico," Francisco answered. "They are from thousands of years ago."

"They must be seven feet tall," Ramon continued as he pointed to one of the bodies.

"All of these statues must have been made from gold brought up from the river that is supposed to be down below," Francisco added as he picked up one of the statues for a closer look.

"We have two more torches left. Let's keep going to see where this cave leads," Ramon suggested as he continued on into the darkness ahead.

What appeared to be an eternity passed as they continued deeper into the cave ahead of them. Gradually the large room they had been in began to become smaller and smaller until they could barely slide through the small opening now between the sides. Looking up at the ceiling they noticed that it was beginning to lower.

"I do not like this," Ramon stopped and announced quietly to Francisco as he tried to search ahead as far as he could see for signs that the cave, which by now was but a crawl space, may increase again in size. But all that could be seen was that the passage would continue to decrease in size. A very noticeable increase in the damp cool air could be felt coming from the small opening ahead. To see farther ahead, Ramon dropped to the floor and stretched his arm out in front of himself, holding the lantern. To his surprise he could tell that there was a continuation of the network of caverns beyond the small opening.

"It gets bigger again ahead of us," Ramon announced to Francisco. "But, it looks like this white rock on the walls has closed the way to get any farther. We would have to break through."

"We must go back outside before the lanterns go out," Francisco suggested.

"You are right," Ramon agreed as he crawled backwards on the cave floor until he could turn around and sit up. "This must be why the Indians found another way."

"I don't think so," Francisco disagreed. "The squaw said this cave was sacred. Probably because of the bodies. It must be some kind of burial tomb."

Ramon said, "I am going to look one more time ahead. Then we will leave." He turned, dropped back to his knees, then crawled ahead as far as he could squeeze himself and still maneuver. Once he reached that point, he reached as far as he could ahead of himself, again with the lantern, for a second and more thorough look. The passageway continued on in front of him but, within a few feet, it turned into a downward direction. On the walls of the passageway into which he looked, he could see what appeared like white popcorn growing on the walls as far as he could see. As white as snow as the walls reflected back in the light of his torch. Ramon then crawled back into the area he had left Francisco, slowly stood up and motioned for him to follow as he headed for the entrance. Soon they reached the area of the Indian bodies that were placed wrapped in animal hides.

"Let's take one of the statues back with us," Ramon suggested as he reached to a point near one of the bodies and grabbed one. "We can then sit down and drink and decide what to do next," he further suggested.

Following a short look back into the passageway, Francisco motioned in agreement and headed for the outside. Unknown to the inexperienced Mexicans, what they had seen within the caves were the bodies of an ancient people. Origin unknown to the Indians created a reason for them to consider the cave system sacred. To the Indians there lay the bodies from which the Spirits they had come to worship had come. The white rock which seemed to grow as a disease on the walls added to the mystery. What they were looking at was calcified deposits left from water dripping and running down the cave walls as it dried.

CHAPTER 9

WITHIN A FEW minutes Francisco and Ramon had reached the entrance. They were surprised to find that night had fallen. Due to a full moon they could immediately see what was their next surprise. The Indian squaw that they had left tied to a cactus was nowhere to be found. Next to the cactus was nothing but the rope they had used to tie her there.

"How the Hell did she get untied?" Ramon exclaimed.

"We must have been followed," Francisco suggested.

"I will go back to the Indian village," Ramon announced. "You go and tell the men that it is time for us to take over the Indians. Be at the village as the sun rises," Ramon instructed.

Without hesitation Ramon headed for the Indian village as Francisco headed back to where the rest of their band of Mexican Desperadoes were camped. Their plan was to enslave the Indians and force them to go to the river within the mountain and retrieve the gold and bring it to them.

As Ramon reached the village he found the Indians had ended their dancing and were sleeping. Though it seemed peaceful to Ramon, the Indians hid the fact that they were well aware of the intentions of the Mexicans. That it meant nothing but trouble ahead for them. However, unknown to Ramon, meetings had transpired between the Indian braves and they had sent two braves to travel a distance that would take several days to the next village to bring back help to rid them of their enemies. The Indians were not only outnumbered but also did not have the guns to fight the Mexicans. Because of what the Mexicans had done by entering the sacred cave, the Indians had no choice but to avenge their Gods and to kill all so as to prevent any of the intruders from leaving the sacred grounds. They had to be given back to their Gods in payment and the statue returned to its place within the cave. Though the Indians were aware of what was to come, there was nothing that they could do until the braves returned with help which was many suns away.

As the first rays of sunlight began to creep across the distant valley, the Mexicans mounted their horses and headed for the nearby village. With guns ready they entered the village and immediately killed several Indians to show their evil intent and strength. Ramon was mounted and waiting as he joined them. Knowing that they were powerless, the Indians grouped themselves and showed no resistance which likely saved many lives.

During the first few days stone buildings were constructed for their housing by the Indians at gunpoint. The first few were slow to be constructed as the Indians had never seen the Mexican way of using three rows of stone for the buildings' walls. The center row of the three acted as the insulator for temperature control within. Another thing needed was a way to make charcoal. In the past the only charcoal they had was what they traded their gold for with the Shoshone in the Panamint Mountain Range west of what is now Death Valley.

The Indians, now slaves of the Mexicans, had to collect enough stackable rocks to make the charcoal kiln. Kilns looked like bee hives and were thirty feet high and in diameter. They had a low arched entrance and back window that were closed with piled rocks when in use. Once a fire was set, the wood was allowed to smolder slowly so as to make the charcoal. Small holes around the kiln base provided the draft.

Many Indians were killed during this time. Most likely for no reason other than to remind them of their existence under the power and control of the Mexicans. The Indians continued to show no resistance. Continued to follow instructions, leaving the Mexicans with no reason to suspect that by now hundreds of Indians were closing in on them. That they would be no match for the joined forces of the two Indian villages.

Much gold was brought up from the river in the days and weeks that followed. Despite the fact that it would take three days to reach the river and return with the gold, much gold was brought up from the river in the following days leading up to the arrival of the additional Indians. Several parties were used to supply gold each day for the smelter in which gold bars were made. Celebration was the daily state of mind amongst the captors as the Indians continued to recover the gold and the bars of pure gold mounted. But justice, unknown to the Mexicans, was soon to come as the Indians from the distant village were near. Hundreds of braves had banded together to come to the aid of their brothers and the salvation of their disturbed Gods.

As night fell once again on the dessert, the Mexicans, as they did each night, gathered around their Padre and knelt in prayer as he spoke. To the Indians, this Padre must have been the Mexicans' God as each time he called they would come to him and pray. Always, as the Indians had noticed, the Padre would carry with him a purse and that he would never put this purse down. Also, from this purse, he would take out a book which he held as they prayed. This, of course, being a bible.

In this purse he also carried important papers including a map that had been drawn showing the exact location of the entrances in the mountain which led to the river below. Before this time only the Indians knew of the location or even of its existence. Now it was of the greatest importance that not one of the Mexicans that knew of its location lived to tell of it. As what was to be their last day ended for the unsuspecting Mexicans, within the shadows of the cactus on a nearby hill, hints of the Indians' purpose soon blended into the night darkness.

So quiet. A soft sound of a breeze. The romancing sound of

distant coyotes was all that could be heard as the darkness of the desert night began its transformation to the soft pink glow of daylight upon the beige sands. A warm feeling of peacefulness prevailed. However, on this day, that peacefulness would not be sustained for long.

Upon the horizon this fateful morning could be seen a thousand Indians in paint as they looked down upon the desperadoes as they slept in quietness. While they slept, the Indians slowly led their way down the steep slope towards the intruders that had invaded their peaceful world and existence in solitude. Nothing could be heard but the whispering wind as it drifted through the early morning sun rays. But, throughout the surrounding cacti the faint shadow of the braves could be seen as they approached. Some crouching, some on hand and knee.

In silence they slowly entered the village. There were enough Indians that several could approach a single tepee and still cover all that were present. None of the braves made a move until all tepees where the Mexicans were sleeping were covered. With a raised arm of their leader, each tepee was entered simultaneously. Immediately screams could be heard breaking the silence with a shiver. Within minutes the Indians dragged their kill from each tepee with scalp in hand.

It took but a few hours for the Indians to wipe out all that were a threat to them and their Gods. But, throughout the remainder of this day, in payment to their Gods, the braves would carry out what would be known as one of the most remembered acts of the Mexican-Indian conflict period in the history of the desert region. To kill their band of intruders would have been satisfactory to the Indians but, for repentance to the Gods, that would not do.

Although only a few hours were required to totally eliminate the desperadoes, the payment to the Gods was yet to begin. All of the Mexican bodies were gathered and laid together side by side. The Indians then proceeded to decapitate and sever all limbs from all of the bodies. As some of the Indians were doing this others were digging a large pit for their bodies to be thrown into. Still more were wandering the surrounding area gathering sage, creosote bush, Pinyon Pine, and dead cactus.

Once this was completed all body parts and the gathered brush were thrown into the prepared pit and set ablaze. As the fire burned the Indians danced in celebration, sang, and smoked locoweed for several hours until the fire burned itself out. This completed their offering to the Gods that had been disturbed by the Mexicans.

As evening approached, the pit was filled and the area returned to look as it was before the Mexicans arrived. With the sun slowly sinking within the distant mountains, what would on any other day have been a feeling of peacefulness in this desert wonder, became a feeling of death. Beneath the slowly dimming light as the day ended, not the slightest indication that the Mexicans had ever entered into this blissful land which had belonged only to the Indians could be noticed. Because the book that the Padre had held appeared to the Indians to be a Godly symbol to the Mexicans, that one item they kept unaware that it also contained the maps that had been drawn of the cave location.

CHAPTER **10**

EARL DORR SAT in silence by the fire amazed at what he had heard as the story White Eagle had been telling came to a conclusion. He stared into the fire as his natural massive imagination carried him into a distant world of thought. To the average individual this story would be overwhelming. However, to a restless ranch hand as young Dorr, it was even beyond that. Remaining silent, Dorr rose from his spot next to the campfire which had become but a faint glow as the darkness of the night had taken its gradual dominance. All that could be seen was the face of White Eagle in the flickering reflection of the fire as he watched his friend wander in amazement and thought.

"Whatever happened after that?" Dorr finally questioned as he broke the silence.

"All returned to as it was before the Mexicans arrived for many seasons," White Eagle responded. "They continued to bring gold up from the river deep within the mountain until one day something happened that changed all that existed for this tribe. Three brothers continued to go within the mountain and descend to the river far below to bring gold to the tribe for trade to others," he continued. "The cave was so vast as the brothers described to the others, that no one knew how far or where it led. Deep within the abyss was a long river and along its banks was the gold that had filtered from above as water seeped into the cavern."

"But, one fateful day ended all that," the old Indian further explained. "While climbing alone on a narrow ledge with only the light of their primitive creosote torch, one brother slipped and fell into the darkness far below. He was never found and because of that all were forbidden to reenter the cursed cave that had swallowed up one of their brothers. Because he was never found the leaders of the tribe believed the brothers had angered the Gods within the mountain," White Eagle concluded. The old Indian then rose from his place by the fire and walked to his nearby horse. He reached into the saddle bag and pulled out what appeared to be an old book. Returning to the warmth of the fire that Dorr had restored, he handed the book to the young cowboy.

"Here. Take this," White Eagle instructed. "This is the prayer book the Mexicans would kneel down for. The map that was in the book was kept by the brothers. The two brothers still alive then went to San Francisco to work at the mines there. That is where they are now," he informed the inquisitive Dorr.

"You go by train to San Francisco and find them," White Eagle further instructed. "You show them you have this and they will give you the map that shows the entrance to the way to the river. Because many years have passed," he continued, "they may be too old to travel with you"

"But why me?" Dorr questioned.

"You my friend," the old Indian replied. "You must go yourself. I am too old to travel with you."

"I can't leave you alone," Dorr pleaded.

"I have been here many winters. This land has been my home since I left the mountain you must go to," he assured Dorr.

"I am sure your father will leave this ranch and meet you at the mountain when you tell him what you plan to do," White Eagle added to reassure Dorr.

Darkness had fallen so it would be morning before Dorr would leave for the ranch house. The following morning Dorr again awoke to the smell of White Eagle's pipe and could see him sitting next to the fire.

"Good morning," White Eagle greeted Dorr as he rose from his bedroll. "Coffee ready for you."

"Thank you," Earl spoke as he reached to fill his cup from the pot hanging over the campfire. "Are you certain that you will not go with me?" Earl asked his friend one more time.

"I cannot go with you," was his only response.

Earl said no more. He knew he could not change his mind.

"The Gods above will be calling me soon. I will stay here on the ranch with your father until then," White Eagle informed the worried cowboy. "You go now to your father."

As instructed, Dorr gathered his belongings. After holding the old Indian in a long bear hug, he mounted his horse and rode from the camp site. At the edge of the clearing he halted his horse and turned to wave. He then proceeded into the distance towards the ranch.

CHAPTER 11

THE MOON HAD begun its peaceful grasp on the horizon as Dorr reached the top of a bluff above the ranch at the edge of the valley below. Unlike the terrain he had spent most of the summer months on, the ranch sat in a valley that was but the bottom of a rolling plain of waving grasses void of but a few trees. Dorr paused for a few moments and scanned the vast view before him as he reminisced the years he had spent on the ranch land where he had been born. Was it time for him to leave? He knew it was.

Darkness of night had fallen as he reached the ranch and led his horse into the barn. He proceeded to remove the saddle and placed it on the floor outside the horse stall. "We will be parting ways, pal," the cowboy said to his horse as he turned and headed for the barn door. "I must travel way too far to take you."

"Hi, Pa," Dorr announced as he entered the ranch house and passed through the sitting room then left without hesitation as he headed for the kitchen for a hot cup of coffee.

"I will be leaving for San Francisco in the morning," Dorr announced as he reentered the sitting room where his father sat.

"White Eagle has been telling you the story, hasn't he?" his father responded.

"Yes. And you can say nothing that will stop me from going. I have had enough of the damn winters in this Hell hole we live in," Dorr answered.

His father did not answer. He knew how his son was. He would not listen to anything he said if he tried to change his mind. Earl was very set in his ways. Not a person easy to please or get along with. Had a mind quick to change and a temper to match. A man happiest when alone.

"He did give you the bible?" he asked his son.

"Yes. He did."

"I have the location of Buck and Oliver, the Indian brothers. At least the last known," Dorr's father informed him as he walked to a desk at the far side of the sitting room.

"That will help you find them. If they have moved on someone there will likely know where they went," he added as he turned from the desk and handed the anxious man the papers.

"Thank you. I will be gone in the morning before the sun rises," Earl informed his father.

"I will leave my horse at the stable in Colorado Springs. You can get him next time you go to town."

With that, he left the room for his bedroom to ready for his trip the following morning. It would not take long to be ready.

"I will take you," his father informed him as the door partly opened.

"If you insist," was his answer his son snorted back.

Before the morning sun rose above the far horizon to announce the arrival of another day, the two were aboard the two horse wagon as they headed for the train station at Colorado Springs about a four hour ride to the southwest.

"I have no reason to stay here much longer. I know you will not return," the elder cowboy broke the silence as the two stood alone waiting for the train to arrive. "You notify me when you know where you will settle and I will come and join you. Maybe your brother Joe will also come," he offered.

"That would be fine," Earl a man of few words, responded.

With a mocking hoot and the screech of the brakes the train announced its approach. The traveler threw his bags onto the luggage car and turned to say goodbye. A quick handshake was all to be had as the horn sounded once again and the wheels squealed as they began to turn. Slowly the train sped up as it traveled from town and began the trip west to San Francisco. Thus began the next chapter of The Legendary Underground River of Gold and a much different life for Earl Dorr. Not being a personable man, he knew it was going to be a long ride from Colorado to San Francisco.

CHAPTER **12**

DESPITE HIS AGE, a young 21, Earl Dorr was ready for the adventure he had ahead of him. He had spent several years living mostly on the open range with his mentor, White Eagle. During these years spending but the hardest months of the winter at the ranch of his father.

The winter of 1906 had passed and Dorr wanted to get to San Francisco as early in the spring as possible to start the next leg of his adventure. That being the train ride from San Francisco to Nipton, California, near Kokoweef Peak. It was unlike the first years of rail travel. Much had changed since the Union and Central Pacific drove the golden spike on May 10th, 1869.

Where the traveler once had to be content with a thorough jolting in a Concord Coach and indifferent care at rough, untidy stage stations, now, in 1906, he was catapulted to luxury. There were the newly invented sleeping coaches called "Pullmans" and "Silver Plate Cars" which live up to their name. They were richly appointed, and had private toilet facilities and were equipped with individual brass spittoons.

Such elegance being beyond the pocketbook of Dorr, presented no problem. There were the unreserved coach accommodations which allowed for great freedom of movement. They were plain, but equipped with a toilet, a coal-burning potbelly stove, hard seats and bunks with straw-filled bags for mattresses. Dining cars were available to all classes, as well as trackside eating places; both offering foods of a standard never known before by the traveling young man.

The journey was to take about seven days, including a scheduled overnight stop in Salt Lake City and Carson City, Nevada. Being the rough soul that he was, Dorr had little interest in the Salt Lake City stop. However, he looked forward with eagerness to the overnight stop in Carson City. He had heard many stories of the famous town and the goings on that he had only imagined.

Dorr was not much for socializing and stayed mostly to himself for the greater part of the trip. He did a fair amount of drinking and card playing, but otherwise watched the new land as it passed by. Sleeping would have been uncomfortable to some. But, to one who spent most of his nights in a bedroll in the elements, it was a pleasant sleep. The swaying of the rail car was even soothing once he became accustomed to it.

One thing that he could not get used to were the kids that seemed to endlessly run wild within the coach which was known as the "modern ship of the plains." He had no use for the noise and commotion. Kids had never been a part of his life. Truth be known, he had little use for people. And, once they got to know him, few people had any use for him.

The stop in Salt Lake City had come and gone and the train continued on its way to the next stop at Carson City. Other than the expected fun Dorr had in mind for Carson City, he had interest in learning more about Christopher "Kit" Carson. Mostly in the 1860's. He had heard many stories of him which included the area in which the mountain that was his final destination was located. Late on day 5 the announcement was made that the train was soon to arrive at Carson City and would remain until the following morning. The sound of the train whistle was a welcome sound to all tiring of the long days of travel.

"Where is there a cheap hotel with a good bar?" Dorr asked the first person he could once his feet hit the ground.

"Your best bet would be the Golden Spur," a boy answered as he was looking to earn money helping people with their luggage. "It is the three-story on the right 10 buildings from here. I can show you," he offered.

"I can find it," Dorr responded gruffly as he threw the boy a quarter.

At that, the young cowboy made his way down the street. Pausing many times, Dorr looked in awe at the buildings. They were like nothing he had ever seen. Much larger and more advanced than Colorado City. The largest city he had seen, Salt Lake City, was larger. He had never left the train there, however. As Dorr continued on the wooden walkway, he looked into all the store windows, stopping at many amazed at their offerings.

Reaching the door to the saloon he stopped to take a final look around, turned toward the door and entered cautiously not knowing what to expect. What he saw was certainly a surprise. There were no girls. There were no tables of gambling. Unlike the saloons in the cattle towns he was used to, this one had no gambling and was not of that atmosphere. Men came here for a restful beer, whiskey or bitters over conversation, or to meet clients and make deals. Some just to play checkers.

There was, to the left as he entered, a very long bar. Likely twenty feet or more at which three well-dressed men stood looking back in his direction with a drink in hand. Behind the bar were several cabinets with glass doors full of liquor bottles nearly to the high ceiling. On the walls were framed paintings of good taste. Mostly of desert scenery or the town itself. The walls were of characteristic paper and the ceilings of formed copper tiles, the likes of which he had never seen. From the ceiling were hung many beautiful crystal chandeliers. Slowly Dorr crossed the polished wooden floor as he approached the bar at which the three men were following his footsteps, cautiously. Behind the bar were two bartenders dressed in white shirts, black vest and pants.

"What might you like to drink?" the man standing closest to him asked.

Dorr remained silent. "What may I order for you?" the man

asked again as Dorr remained.

"You are not from these parts, are you?" the man inquired. Slowly Dorr looked up as he turned his head and looked at the man.

"No. I am not. Why? Is it that I am not dressed as you are?" Dorr questioned sharply, dressed in his usual cowboy attire.

"No," the man answered. "Because a respectful stranger does not refuse an offer of a drink when given by a gentleman of the town."

"I believe that would be a whiskey. Thank you," Dorr responded following a few moments of silence as the two looked into each other's eyes.

"Are you packing a gun?" the bartender questioned.

"I do have one in my baggage," Dorr responded carefully.

"Just keep it there," the bartender warned.

"I will. I have no use for it here," Dorr obliged.

"What is your business here?" the other man at the bar inquired as he slid closer to where Dorr was leaning on one elbow on the bar.

"Just passing through," Dorr responded cautiously as he turned his head to make eye contact with the stranger. Following a couple of hours and several drinks, Dorr left the saloon and new acquaintances and walked to the hotel which was but two buildings back towards the train station. The hotel was at one time an inn, hub for business deals and a civic center in whose dining room politicians orate, townsmen enjoy community dances, and even occasional funerals are held. Each bedroom, furnished with a wash basin, bowl and pitcher, chamber pot, chair, and smoky kerosene lamp, was a cubicle partitioned with walls of brown paper-- all the guests can hear one another. There was no bath. To bathe, one must go to the bathhouse in the building next to the hotel. It was but a few minutes and Dorr was sleeping soundly.

CHAPTER 13

THE SUN WAS just rising as Dorr awoke following the two un-eventful days of travel since the train pulled out of Carson City. During the two days of travel from Carson City Dorr had learned in conversations with the railroad attendant in his car that the company, The Sanborn Map Company, for which the Peysert brothers worked, likely had their office in Oakland. Oakland was the end of the old California and Nevada Railroad Line. Stopping in Oakland would save Dorr from having to change trains to continue to San Francisco.

The train attendant had no idea about the Indian brothers but did know that Sanborn Company had leased the old California-Nevada Railroad East Bay Station on San Pablo Avenue in Oakland. So, Dorr had a good place from which to start his search.

"Good luck, to you," the railroad attendant wished Dorr as he departed the train with travel bag in hand.

"Thank you very much for all your help," Dorr returned to the attendant with a wave of his hat as he turned and slowly walked from the train.

The train station was massive in comparison to any building he had ever seen. Only two stories, it sprawled to consume the entire city block. Also, in appearance constructed in Spanish masonic, light sand color. An impressive sight for the mountain man.

All Dorr had seen in amazement soon would be erased as soon as he walked into the main street in front of the station. As far as he could see were two and three story buildings. People everywhere. Horses pulling carriages, wagons loaded with provisions, covered wagons, and even a few wagons running by themselves.

Dorr walked the short distance to the building where he was told he could find Sanborn Map Company. It was a few blocks along the tracks in an area called Elmhurst. At least in this area there were a few adult trees remaining to the pleasure of Dorr.

"Can I help you?" a voice could be heard as he entered a small office filled with pigeon hole shelves full of rolled papers and tables with drawings everywhere.

"I am looking for Buck and Oliver Peysert. I was told they work here," Dorr replied to the still hidden source of the voice.

"They are not here now" was his response as he moved towards the voice. Finally he could see a man bent over one of the tables working on a map in progress.

"You will find them at 14th and San Pablo. They are redrawing for the addition of the new First National Bank Building there," the man responded without looking up from his work. "You can walk it. About one mile straight down the street."

"Thank you for your help," Dorr said as he turned and headed for the door. After pausing for a response never to come, he exited back onto the street. The walk seemed much longer than a mile and the cowboy hated every step. People everywhere. All over the street, wooden walkway, hanging out windows and standing on crowded balconies. After passing a Wells Fargo building, billiard parlor, barber, horseshoe and horse stalls, mercantile, and many more, he could see a large building under construction at the next street intersection. Standing at what looked like seven or eight stories, it was quite a sight. He had never seen anything over two stories high.

At the street intersection he could see a few men standing together talking and looking at the building. Some were looking at the streets and pointing in various directions. As Dorr approached the group of men he could see that none of them were of Indian descent. He then noticed two loading equipment onto a large wagon. They were of Indian descent.

"Are you men Oliver and Buck?" Earl inquired as he approached the men loading the wagon. Without a word spoken, both men stopped working and turned and stared with bewilderment on their faces.

"White Eagle told me to find you. He said you have a map he wants you to give me," Dorr finally said as he broke the silence.

"You have the bible the Padre carried the maps in?" one of the Indian brothers questioned Dorr.

"Yes I do," Earl answered as he presented the bible that was in a tote bag he was carrying.

One of the Indians reached into a mail pouch attached to a leather strap and hanging loosely around his neck and pulled out a paper. Without a word he handed it to Dorr. The young cowboy looked at the paper handed to him and could see that it was the map White Eagle described.

"You go now. The Gods will protect you," one of the Indians ordered.

"Will you be coming to join us?" Earl questioned. "My father and brother Joe will be as soon as I find a ranch that I think they would like."

"We might. We talk to your father when he gets there," one of the Indian brothers responded. "We can do a lot to help. But, still cannot go into the mountain."

"I know," Dorr responded. "But, that is O.K."

That was the only conversation between them. Dorr turned and walked away.

Next would be another long train ride to Nipton, California, in the middle of the Mojave Desert and yet another chapter of true adventure for Earl Dorr. Whatever the future was to be, it would suit Dorr much better than the hustle of the city. This was evident by the haste in his step as he headed directly back to the train station.

"How soon can I get the Hell out of this place?" he asked as he reached the ticket window.

The route to Nipton was a much more indirect route than Colorado to San Francisco. Santa Fe would get him to Sacramento. The Northern Pacific would take him to Bakersfield, California, and the Central Pacific to Ivanpah, California. Not far from Nipton. If all went well, a ten day trip.

After the train had pulled out of the Oakland station, Dorr settled into his seat and began to look over what he had received from the Indian brothers. Along with several maps he found that there also were many notes written the Mexicans, the Indian elders, and later by Oliver, Buck and George Peysert. It took some time for Earl to fully understand the meaning of notes written by the Mexicans and the elders. However, he easily understood the notes of the brothers who had received the same education as Earl when they worked at his father's ranch from 1880 until 1902. His father had hired a teacher who lived with them. Not known by Earl until reading the notes, was that in 1903 Oliver, Buck, and a third brother George had returned to the site of the massacre and, using the maps, had relocated the entrance and entered the underground caverns as described by the Indian elders.

At some time between 1903 and 1905 the three brothers spent a six week period in the caverns. During the six week excursion brother George died from a fall from which his body could not be recovered off the bank of the underground river, later to be known as the "Kokoweef Underground River of Gold." It was told that George had dived into the river on the cavern floor and had struck an unseen rock. Because his body could not be recovered, Indian beliefs would not permit them to reenter the caverns. Oliver and Buck Peysert were then forced to leave the mountain and their brother George to the Spirits of Kokoweef Mountain. The brothers had planned to continue at some point to San Francisco because of the good job opportunities there.

Prior to George's death the brothers carried lumber to the

cavern floor and constructed a sluice box and, using a pump, the three mined for six weeks. What they had retrieved in the six weeks in the cavern turned out to be worth $57,000 at $20 per once if they had sent their gold directly to the United States mint for assay. Though not indicated in their notes, they must have left the gold in the caverns, likely where they found it by the underground river. Dorr was amazed at the amount of gold the three could recover in such a short time.

As the train stopped for water and supplies in Sacramento, Earl decided to forward this information to his father and suggest to his father that he and his brother Joe close up the ranch in Colorado and meet him in Nipton. Also suggesting that his father contact Oliver and Buck Peysert and that he knew they could not enter the cavern or the area of Kokoweef Peak but could help develop a ranch in Nipton with his father and be near to give supportive information.

As the train pulled out of Sacramento, Dorr had only dreaming to do for the next several days hoping that when he arrived in Nipton he would have good news.

CHAPTER **14**

THE TRAIN RIDE to Ivanpah, California, turned out to be a very long and tedious journey across what seemed to be an endless sea of sand and rock as they entered the very hot desert now known as the Mojave. Following several days the first town of any size, Bakersfield, could be seen as the early morning sun began to rise above the distant hills. With its population of nearly 3000, the town appeared very out of place after days of nothing but sand and cactus. Bakersfield had been settled in 1860 by a German by the name of Christian Bohug to supply miners in the area. However, in 1862 the town was destroyed by a flash flood. Within a year, and with the arrival of the California gold rush as it advanced into the desert from the mountains to the north, Thomas Baker moved the settlement from the banks of the Kern River where it had been and the town flourished due to the mining, the railroad, and developing oil industry. Though the train would be in Bakersfield only two hours to receive water and supplies, at least it allowed a small amount of time to depart.

In what appeared to be no time at all, the train's whistle could be heard as being the signal it was time to return. The next leg of the journey was two more days of the same-- sand, heat, and the occasional Indian or miner on horseback as they waited for the train to pass to continue on to an unknown destination.

On the second day out of Bakersfield the train entered the settlement of Baker, which would be the last town of any size Earl Dorr would see for a long time. The length of which really was not a concern to this man of a nature that did not fit into the general way of life. Dorr would sooner shun any situation or anybody with whom he could not be in complete control.

Barstow, Dorr likely could fit into if his purpose would allow him to stay. In the late 1880's, the Barstow area became a mining center. The small town of Daggett, 5 miles downriver, was founded in 1860. It was originally called Calico Junction but was renamed after California Lieutenant Governor John Daggett when silver was discovered 6 miles north in the Calico Mountains in 1882. The finding of silver in Calico and the building of the Southern Pacific Railroad from Mojave to Daggett in 1882 made the area a major mining area. The 20 mule teams came into being when teams of ten horses were hitched together with two wagons and a water wagon to haul ore from Daggett to the town of Calico. Daily wagon runs from the town of Ryan to the north would also arrive through Greenwater Valley carrying upwards of 39,000 pounds of borax ore each.

The Calico Railroad started hauling ore from Calico to the Ore Grande Milling Company across the river from Daggett in 1888. That same year, the Santa Fe Railroad arrived. The mine was shut down in 1896 when the silver had played out. But in 1883 the borax rush had hit Calico, and by 1902, Daggett and Calico had diminished and Barstow had turned into the mining and railroad center of the entire desert area. The stop was short and within a couple of hours the train was once again moving on towards Ivanpah.

Dorr could not believe what he first saw when the train pulled into Ivanpah at first light the following day. There was absolutely nothing of a town. All that existed was a water tower and one building serving many purposes along with a small stable. Here Dorr was to stay until late in the day to catch a Wells Fargo stage to finish the final leg of the trip to Nipton ten miles north. He stood for several moments and searched the area in all directions. It mattered not which direction he looked. They all looked the same-- more sand and rock with mountains in the distance. Finally he turned to cross the tracks which were now empty, as the train had left, and walked to the nearest of the two buildings which were side by side about twenty feet from the tracks. As he entered the light brown stucco building he could see a bar on the further side of the room that looked very welcoming.

"I would like a shot of Wild Turkey backed up with another, please," he instructed the man behind the bar.

"Yes sir," was his response as the man placed an open bottle on the bar in front of Dorr.

"Where are you headed?" he inquired.

"I am heading to find a small ranch or something near Nipton for my family and then head into the mountains," Dorr replied.

"A lot of mining in that area," the man informed Dorr as he handed him another drink.

"Where did you come in from?"

"San Francisco."

"Shit. You must have just missed a very big earthquake that destroyed most of the city about two weeks ago."

"Damn. Can you telegraph? I must inform my father in Colorado."

"Yes. What do you want it to say?" the man said as he readied his pen.

"Will be in Nipton by tomorrow. Contact Oliver and Buck as soon as you can. You and brother Joe shut down the ranch and come here. I need you," Dorr instructed him. "I will send another when I get to Nipton. Can find a ranch in Nipton area."

"How long until the coach arrives for Nipton?" Earl inquired as he reached and lifted the bottle that had been placed in front on him.

"Only about two hours," he replied.

"My name is Robert. Nice to meet you," the bartender offered.

"I am Earl. Plan to be in the area quite some time."

"Planning to file a claim?" he further explored into what Dorr's intentions were.

"Sort of," was all that Dorr would offer.

"I know only of one other passenger coming in on the stage," Robert informed Earl as he placed a second beer on the counter. "It is a female traveling by herself."

"Odd place for a girl to be traveling alone," Dorr commented.

"I hear she is quite a lady. Her name is Pearl Hart," Robert continued. "She is coming in from Kansas City. Rumor has it that she spent time in Yuma Prison for something."

"Well. That ought to be interesting," Earl commented slyly.

"Do you have a shower so I can freshen up a bit?"

"Sure. I will get you a towel and soap," the attendant offered as he reached under the counter and handed it to Dorr.

"Thank you. One more drink for the shower," Earl thanked him and turned to head for the door in the back of the room.

After his shower he returned and backed up his drink with another whiskey as he waited out the hour that was left until the stagecoach was to arrive.

Pearl Hart, arriving on the coach coming in and joining Earl, had, in fact, spent time in Yuma State Prison for armed robbery of a Wells Fargo stage.

CHAPTER 15

"I CAN HEAR the stage approaching," Robert suddenly announced as he headed from behind the bar to the front door.

"Come on, Earl. I will introduce you to the driver and Ms. Hart."

"Right behind you," Earl obliged as he rose from his chair and followed Robert outside just as the coach arrived.

This would be the first experience Dorr had with the impressive Concord stagecoach. His travel before this trip across country was by horse. In the ranch country of Colorado it would be work wagons for carrying supplies. The Concord stagecoach was used extensively in the west due to its design in addition to being exported to Australia and Africa. The model now arriving had a twelve foot wheel base and weighed in the vicinity of 2100 pounds. The coach itself rode on twin through braces made of rawhide strips which made a three inch leather spring. The undercarriage was painted bright yellow but the coach body color was scarlet red and green.

"Welcome to the City of Ivanpah," Robert greeted Pearl Hart with an extended hand as she stepped from the coach.

"This coach will be your coach to Nipton so your bags may stay on during your short stay," Robert informed her.

"Thank you," she replied as she allowed Robert to assist her from the coach.

"This is Earl Dorr. He will be riding with you for the short trip to Nipton where you will be able to stay until the train to Globe, Arizona, arrives," Robert informed her. "That will be an overnight stay. It arrives there tomorrow morning."

Pearl Hart 1899

Pearl hid the fact well that she was, indeed, a woman. From her cowgirl boots to her Stetson hat she dressed as a cowhand. But, beneath it all, was a lady. Black hair tucked beneath her hat, gray blue eyes, barely one hundred pounds and a height of five foot two.

"Would you join me at my table for a drink or coffee while we wait for the horses to rest," Earl offered Pearl.

"That would be very nice," she replied with a soft voice which did not match her demeanor.

"Would you please make that a whiskey from the top shelf," she requested as she left to freshen up a bit.

"Robert, whiskey and make it the best you have," Earl ordered as he turned towards Robert as he entered the room.

"Coming right up," he replied. "Careful, Earl. She might bite."

"That's O.K., it has been a long time since I've been bitten," Earl replied back with a smile on his face.

Within a few minutes Pearl returned and accepted Earl's offer as he pulled a chair out for her to sit.

"You look tired and bothered," Earl said as he broke the silence and watched her empty her glass of whiskey in what seemed one swallow.

"I am both," Pearl replied. "I am sure this whiskey will make it possible for me to nap from here to Nipton during the six hour ride," she replied as she lifted the glass Earl had refilled.

"I just have a lot on my mind and it has been a long ride," she offered.

It was not long before the driver of the stagecoach opened the door and announced that it was time to board for the ride to Nipton.

"We had better get going," Earl said as he stood by Pearl's chair with his hand extended in offer to assist her from her chair.

Pearl took Earl's hand in acceptance, thanking him as they started to walk to the stagecoach together. The door window was glazed but the side windows were unglazed. Canvas or leather curtains hung above each window which could be rolled down during bad weather. Plush interiors had three upholstered bench seats that allowed up to twelve passengers to ride inside. There was also one bench seat on the outside rear of the coach for an additional two passengers.

But, this ride was solely for Earl and Pearl. Earl, being a gentle-man on the inside, assisted Pearl into the stage coach and then placed himself in the seat across from her. It was a silent ride. As she had said, the whiskey would allow her to nap for the short ride to Nipton.

CHAPTER 16

TWO PRIMARY WAGON trails crossed, one Tucson to San Francisco, the other Los Angeles to Denver, in this wide desert valley marking the spot where the town of Nipton would take form in the 1870's. The settlement evolved, over time, with the ever-changing characters that lived and worked in the Ivanpah Valley.

On January 1st, 1900, a gold seeker from Pennsylvania named Sam D. Karns, staked what is believed to be the first mining claim in the area and called it Nappeno. With the staking of adjacent claims such as the Susquehana, Cumberland, Northhumberland, Pennsylvania, and the Osceola, they were combined within the Crescent District and called The Nippeno Consolidated Mine. The miners took up residence here at the crossroads, which became known as Nippeno Camp. Soon the town boasted a railroad station, hotel, and stage coach stop. The town of Nipton was born on February 5th, 1905, with the arrival of the first train on the newly constructed San Pedro, Los Angeles, and Salt Lake City Railroad.

The sleeping Dorr woke up as the coach slowed upon entering the town of Nipton.

"Time to wake up," Dorr announced as he reached across to Pearl's seat and tapped her on the shoulder.

She awoke with a start but soon realized that it was but the arrival to town that she had encountered.

"I am sorry. I did not mean to frighten you," Earl apologized.

"That is alright," Pearl assured him. "I am just a bit nervous."

"Are you staying at the hotel?" Earl inquired.

"I do not have a plan as yet," she replied.

"I will be staying at the hotel. May I get a room for you?" Earl offered.

"I do not have the money to stay there. But thank you," she replied.

"Don't worry about it. I will take care of it. You must stay somewhere."

"You are a nice man, but I want my own room" Pearl informed.

"Of course," Earl replied with a glance and smile as he approached the clerk's desk.

As he waited for the clerk, he glanced about the lobby. Quite impressive for a place in the middle of nowhere. Complete with a Victorian look of decorative chairs, carpet and even a chandelier.

"May I help you?" the clerk announced from behind the desk.

Dorr turned to find a man about the size of Pearl with thick glasses looking back at him.

"Yes. I would like two rooms please. Adjoining, if possible," Earl requested.

"I do have two with a view of Main Street," the clerk informed him. "Would that be satisfactory?"

"That would be wonderful, thank you," Earl acknowledged.

After paying for the rooms and securing the keys he walked to where Pearl was standing looking out the front window towards the rather busy street.

"I have the rooms. Let me help you with your bag," he offered as he motioned towards the staircase which led to the rooms on the next floor above.

He opened the door to the first room allowing Pearl to enter. Following her he placed her bag on the floor next to the bed.

"I have the room next to yours if you need anything," Earl informed her. "How about I take you to dinner about six and then we can walk to see what the town looks like," Earl offered.

"That would be wonderful. Why are you being so nice to a stranger?" Pearl asked with a slight tilt of her head.

"Tell you what," Earl began his reply. "I am alone in a strange town just as you are. I can see a nice, but hurting, person hidden inside you somewhere. There is no reason for either one of us being alone."

"You do have a way with words, don't you," she replied looking Earl straight in the eyes.

With a slight hug of assurance, Earl turned and walked to the door.

"See you at six," he said as he turned and closed the door behind him.

Before retiring for a little sleep himself as it was only about two in the midafternoon, Earl left the hotel and walked to the rail station to get the time for Pearl's train to Searchlight, Nevada, then Globe, Arizona, and to send a message to Colorado to inform his father of his arrival. It was but a short walk past the Town Hall and the Nipton Trading Post, which was basically a general mercantile. Just across the dirt main street was the Searchlight and Nipton Freight and Stage Office behind which was the train depot and telegraph office. Earl sent off his message to his father along with a strong encouragement to leave for Nipton as soon as he could. He inquired and found that there would be no train for two days that would take Pearl to her destination. It was not to his disappointment.

"Thank you for your help," Earl thanked the attendant. "Looks like I will be staying around Nipton for a while."

"I am Ralph," the man behind the desk introduced himself. "Anything you need just ask. I will be glad to help you. It is a small town. We will see plenty of each other."

"I am certain that I will need plenty of help, thank you," Earl said as he tipped his hat, turned and walked out the door. Returning to his room he immediately undressed and laid down for a long awaited restful nap.

CHAPTER 17

REALIZING THE TIME was fast approaching that he was to meet Pearl, Earl quickly arose from the bed upon awakening and headed straight for the bathroom for a fast bath. Meanwhile, Pearl had readied herself and decided to venture to Earl's room. What Earl was to see was nothing like what she had looked like earlier. She had really reclaimed her femininity. Her long black hair flowed over her shoulders to her mid-back. In her hair she pinned a white rose she borrowed from an arrangement in her room which brought attention to a small white lace hat. Her white short-sleeve dress was lined gracefully with lace. Her boots were replaced with laced black shoes.

After knocking, twice, and receiving no response, she slowly opened the door to Earl's room and poked her head in through the small opening. Seeing nothing but an empty bed, Pearl entered the room and closed the door. Hearing Earl in the washroom, she decided to sit in a chair that was on the far side of the room with a view of the main street and wait.

It was not long and Earl entered the bedroom from the washroom and walked in the direction away from where Pearl was sitting to where his bag sat in a chair. Back to her, he proceeded to gather his shaving gear and union suit from it.

Leaving his union suit next to his bag on the chair, he turned to the wash basin to shave utilizing the mirror above. As he looked into the mirror to shave he froze in a stare as Pearl's image slowly went from imaginary to reality. Too late to do anything else the totally nude Earl reached for the only thing he could reach. His union suit. Before he could turn to face her he could hear her muffled laughter.

Pearl Hart Seated in Dress

"Very nice," she finally said breaking the silence. "Best thing that I have seen for a long time."

"Would you like a closer look?" Earl asked sounding irritated at Pearl but in reality only embarrassed as he slowly turned to face her holding his union suit hanging in front of him.

"No. Not now. That was fine," she replied with a wide smile.

Earl turned, and willingly flashing his ass, finished shaving. In silence Pearl sat and watched as he shaved and dressed for the evening. As he finished dressing, Pearl rose from her place in the chair. For the first time Earl could see the new Pearl.

"Holy shit," he exclaimed. "Where the Hell did you come from. Where and why did you hide the beauty I am now looking at?" he continued shaking his head slightly. "You are beautiful."

"And I am hungry," Pearl notified him.

"O.K., let's go eat," Earl said as he reached for her hand to guide her to the door.

Hand in hand they walked the distance from the room to the stairs to the lobby below. As they reached the top of the stairs, Earl motioned Pearl to walk down next to the rail so she could hold on to it as he followed her to the bottom level.

"You can tell that there has been a lot of recent work done on the inside of the hotel," Pearl mentioned, "but I can see a lot of areas of improvement that could still be done," she commented.

"Looks nice to me as it is," Earl replied. "But, who am I to know? Being as I have lived but on a ranch in the backwoods of Colorado all my life."

They continued to walk through the lobby towards the eating area as they looked throughout taking in each other's comment. The dining room consisted of but three tables though there was room for several more. A man approached their table, dressed as if he had just left the kitchen, where he must have also been cooking and cleaning the dishes, took their order politely, and returned to the kitchen.

"This does not seem to be a very well-run hotel, does it," Pearl commented after the man had left the room.

"Seems like any other place I have been to," Earl replied raising a quiet snicker out of Pearl.

"You appear to have had some experience with hotels," Earl commented.

"Kind of," Pearl agreed.

"How about going for a walk after we eat," Pearl suggested trying to change the subject.

"Sounds good to me," Earl agreed.

As they finished their dinner, they thanked the waiter and returned to the lobby.

"Would you please excuse me? I would like to get my wrap. It may be chilly outside," Pearl requested.

"Of course. I will be right here," Earl assured her.

Earl watched as she walked up the stairs and until she entered her room. He then sat and looked about the lobby noticing several pictures on the walls of desert scenery and a small town of questionable quality buildings.

"Are those pictures of this town?" Earl asked the man behind the hotel desk.

"Yes. Of the town when the first buildings were built and of some of the mines in the area," he replied not lifting his eyes from his paperwork.

Earl then looked above in response to the sound of a door closing and stood in wait for Pearl as she descended the stairs.

"Thank you," Pearl said as she placed her arm through Earl's outstretched arm. "Let's go for our walk," Earl offered as he opened the front door.

"Looks like a nice evening for one," Pearl commented as they reached the wooden boardwalk that passed in front of the hotel, as well as the other buildings on the immediate street which included nearly all business buildings within the entire town. Beyond Main Street consisted of mostly residences, outhouses, tents, and storage sheds.

CHAPTER 18

"THERE IS A small park with a bench and a light down by the train station I noticed when I went there to send a message to family and to check on the train schedule for you. How about we walk there and maybe sit and talk for a while," Earl suggested.

"That sounds fine," Pearl agreed.

"What did you find out about the train schedule?" she inquired.

"There will be no train that you can take for two days," Earl replied. "I hope that works out to your pleasure."

"I am not sure when I want to leave anyway," Pearl informed Earl. "I may like to stay for a while."

They continued in silence walking towards the park, Earl hoping Pearl did not see the sly smile that crossed his face with the news. As they walked towards the park they passed a small empty building that was a boarding house before the hotel opened. It had been closed since. Beside the closed boarding house was a theater which looked as if it still was used occasionally. Then a mercantile followed by a hardware store.

"Why don't we walk on the other side of the street where the horse corral and the blacksmith shop is," Earl suggested as they approached the saloons that were very lively to say the least. "I do not know the town well enough yet to chance walking you past these saloons at night."

"I think that would be a good idea," Pearl agreed as she looked at the two passed-out men lying on the boardwalk ahead. Behind were the saloons from within which could be heard the drunkards and loud arguing. Once past the blacksmith shop they reached the railroad and stage station followed by the telegraph office beside which was the park. Sitting on the only bench, they could look beyond into the distant valley and mountains that shined under the silver light of the full moon.

"Nice and quiet here with the station buildings between us and the saloons," Earl commented to break the silence which had fallen over them.

"Tell me about yourself, please Earl," Pearl requested as she looked up into the man she had befriended. "I am developing feelings for you and I don't even know anything about you."

"Why are you?" Earl asked.

"I am not sure, really," Pearl replied. "I just feel very comfortable with you and I need a friend."

"I hope I am not wrong trusting in you," Pearl added.

"Well, I feel I am in the same situation," Earl injected. "I think we must tell of one another. To assure each other if what we are heading into is what we really want. Neither one of us came to this country with the main objective being to fall into a binding relationship. We both have other important intentions."

Pearl agreed as she listened to Earl very intently as he spoke with a nod of her head.

"I really think we can accomplish what we need to do and also test our feelings for one another if we are honest with each other," Earl continued. "We can only do that by telling one another who we are."

"That is true," Pearl agreed. "I have a lot to tell. A lot I told myself I would never tell or speak of again."

"I am certain that you will not like a lot of what I must tell you," she ventured on. "But, I must to be true to you thinking that I am being fully honest. I just must take a chance that you will understand and give me a chance."

"You are starting to worry me," Earl spoke up shyly. "I will tell you of me first for there is not much to say."

He proceeded to tell Pearl all that White Eagle had told him which would explain why he had come to Nipton. He told her of his family, the ranch in Colorado, and that his father and brother would be arriving soon. He told her what his plans were about the underground river.

"You see," Earl concluded, "I am really just like most men, nothing special."

"I have experience that tells me that you are not like most men," Pearl disagreed.

"I guess it must be my turn," she started, looking at Earl then rubbing her head and looking towards the ground before her.

"Please try to understand. Let me finish. Then I promise to answer any questions you may have."

"I am no fool," he assured her. "I will not prejudge you about anything you say without allowing you all the opportunity in the world to explain. This is not to judge you. I want to know you so I can be free to develop feelings for you."

CHAPTER **19**

"WELL, HERE GOES," Pearl began. "It is a long story," she warned.

"That is alright," Earl assured her. "I am in no hurry sitting here with you."

"I was born in Ontario, Canada." Knowing that she was older than Earl, she went on by the year that she was born. She hid it well. She looked several years younger than she really was.

Pearl's mind drifted as she remembered watching the world pass by her railcar window on her trip with a destination of Trinidad, Colorado. A tear appeared in her eye and cascaded over her cheek, landing on her blouse. This was not the way it was to be. All she ever wanted was to be free of all the overbearing controls of the Catholic boarding school and the abusive men that had torn her life apart. All she wanted was to be free to live as she wanted and to be able to go where she could find the peace that she longed for. She never imagined how long that road was going to be.

1888, Ontario, Canada

Pearl knew she was pregnant. She knew her boyfriend would be there soon. He was already late to meet her by the school. He promised to walk her home for her weekend pass.

"Hi, Pearl," Frank said as he approached from behind her and placed his hands on her hips.

"Hi, Frank. I have something that I must tell you," Pearl responded quietly.

"What is wrong?" Frank questioned as he sensed her concern.

"I am pregnant. I know I am. I am never past my time," Pearl responded.

"Get married," Frank responded immediately. "Your mother and father have never approved of me and sure won't now. You hate that school you go to."

"But, what can I do? I am only sixteen. We have no money."

"You don't have to worry," Frank tried to assure her. "I will take care of you and the baby. I have changed. The baby and no job would have been too much but, not now. We can go to Chicago. I know that I can get a job there. The World Columbian Exposition is there now. There are many jobs."

"I will give you one chance because of the baby," Pearl responded sternly looking Frank straight in the eye. "If you hit me once you will never see me again." Frank Hart had a reputation as a hot-headed, semi-professional gambler, sometime bartender, and full time drinker, who had spent more time nursing hangovers than working.

Pearl did go home and tell her mother. She made her promise not to tell her father until she was well out of town. He was one for her to fear. Her mother knew that he had hit Pearl on several occasions, but, had no idea of the sexual abuse that Pearl had been subjected to. Inside, Pearl had no idea if the baby was Frank's or her father's. A secret she must live with.

Frank and Pearl did get married by a local judge and secretly left for Chicago with no one knowing but her mother. Finding a job was not as easy as Frank had thought. However, he did soon become a barker, standing outside one of the exhibits announcing the show in hopes of attracting people.

"I know that does not pay much," Frank assured Pearl. "It will pay the bills until I find something better."

The following six months were not better. Pearl had her baby, a girl. Frank had not hit Pearl but had returned to gambling and drinking heavily again. Pearl began to feel the fear as before.

Pearl lay in bed. It was late and she knew that he was likely to be drunk. That was when she feared him the most. Her only feeling of security was knowing she had saved enough money to send the baby to her mother and purchase a train ticket to somewhere far from his reach. The sound of the door closing caused Pearl to shiver. She could hear Frank stumbling in the dark.

"You are drunk again," Pearl yelled. "Have you any money to feed the baby?"

"You shut your damn mouth," Frank yelled back.

"You promised me that this would stop," Pearl exclaimed.

"I will show you what I promised," Frank yelled as he walked to the end of the bed.

Frank pulled the screaming Pearl from the bed. Her head could be heard hitting the floor. The screaming continued along with the thump of repeated hitting. Frank left the room leaving Pearl on the floor bleeding about her mouth and nose. She lay quietly crying in the dark room. Pearl had learned from, and had become inspired by, Annie Oakley and Bell Starr, watching their shows at the Exposition. Fearing when the hitting would start again, Pearl left unannounced and took the next train west. The first destination would be Trinidad, Colorado, a place where she could start over by herself in her continuing search for peace in her life.

CHAPTER 20

THE TRAIN SLOWED as it arrived at Trinidad, Colorado. Pearl had stayed with Frank as long as she dared and her desire to strike out on her own prevailed giving her peace of mind in sending her baby to her mother. The train squealed to a stop. Pearl gathered her luggage and left the train. Standing on the station platform, she looked around and spotted a hotel in the distance a short way down the dirt street. She cautiously entered the hotel lobby and approached the man at the desk. The clerk slowly lifted his head and looked silently at Pearl.

"I would like a room," Pearl finally requested.

"That will be two dollars for the room and fifty cents to bathe."

"I need both, thank you," Pearl responded. "Do you know where I may find a job?"

"Doing what?" the clerk asked.

"I can sing."

"Try the Valverde Saloon," he suggested. "They need someone that can sing or dance. Both would be a plus."

"Thank you," Pearl said with a smile as she slowly handed the man his money.

Pearl climbed the stairs to her room which was on the second level. Finding the door with the right room number on it, Pearl opened it curiously. She spotted the bed and as she scanned the room, placed her bags gently upon it. Pushing the bags to the further side, Pearl lay on the bed and closed her eyes. She was now alone. In spite of it all, she was scared. Not knowing why, she began to cry. It could be fear, reality of being alone, or reality of being safe from Frank. Years with Frank had left scars, inside and out. He had made her feel as if she were useless. Not a whole person.

The following morning Pearl dressed and started to show herself how wrong Frank was by shopping at the nearby stores for appropriate clothes to look for a job at the Valverde saloon. She obtained a hairstyle that was fitting and a complete Victorian outfit, including a hat and shoes.

The cut-glass door of the Valverde Saloon swung open and a beautifully dressed woman walked in. It was the new Pearl. Though nervous, Pearl managed a demanding voice.

"I would like to speak to the boss."

"For what?" the man behind the bar responded.

"Personal," Pearl answered.

"He ain't in," he answered sharply.

"Then I will wait."

"I am Mr. Burke," a man in a gray suit with dark stripes spoke up as he approached Pearl from the back of the room.

"Are you the boss?" Pearl inquired.

"I am the owner. What is it that you want, my dear?"

"A job, please."

"And what can you do for me?" Mr. Burke inquired.

"I can sing and I can dance," Pearl informed him.

"I am sure you can. But, I have all the girls that I need. Sorry," he responded as he turned and walked back to the table he was sitting at in the back of the room.

Pearl approached a man who was playing a piano nearby. "Do you know how to play 'Arkansas Traveler'?"

"Sur' do Lady," the piano player responded. "Would you like me to play it?"

"Please."

Without hesitation the piano player started playing. Pearl climbed the three stairs onto the stage and immediately started to sing along with the music as she had done in Chicago. Hearing

Pearl singing, Mr. Burke looked up from the table and listened. He remained at the table for a few minutes. But, as soon as Pearl began to attract the attention of some of the saloon patrons around the stage, Mr. Burke became interested. He pushed himself through the men around the stage and approached Pearl. Pearl finished her song and despite the calls from the men to continue, responded to Mr. Burk's hand gestures and followed him to his office.

"Please sit down on the sofa," he told Pearl. Pearl sat as requested.

"Are you comfortable, there?" My Burke inquired.

"Yes sir. Thank you," Pearl spoke softly.

"Would you like a drink?"

"It has been a dry day," Pearl answered. "Bourbon would be nice if you have it."

"I do have it," he assured her as he lifted a bottle and filled a glass. He reached out to Pearl offering the glass.

"Thank you, sir," Pearl said with a nod and smile.

"Do you do anything but sing?"

"I also dance."

"Anything else?"

"What else would you want me to do?"

Mr. Burke approached Pearl and sat. "Anything that keeps the customers happy," was his answer.

Pearl stood and turned to face Mr. Burke. "I am certain that I qualify."

Pearl downed the rest of the drink with one swallow, put the glass on the table, tipped her hat, turned to leave the room, but stopped.

"What time would you like me here?" she inquired.

"About seven."

"About seven it will be," Pearl assured him as she exited the room.

Pearl did return that evening and most of the evenings during the next few months. During that time she gained a large and loyal following. That lasted about six months. Then she found herself being attracted to a customer by the name of Joe Boot. Following one of her shows, Joe surprised Pearl with an invitation. "This town is beginning to get on my nerves. Why don't you come with me to Globe, Arizona. That is where I am going. Back to the mines where I belong."

"But, what would I do there?" Pearl asked.

"Same as you are doing here. Or you could cook. The miners get real hungry," Joe replied.

It would not be long and Pearl did leave Trinidad with Joe. But, when she got to Phoenix, Arizona, and saw the city, she decided to stay as Joe continued on to Globe.

"I really want to stay here at least for a while," Pearl informed Joe.

"That is O.K. but I have had enough of the city life," Joe replied. "The mines are rich in gold, silver and copper. I know I can strike it rich there. I know nothing else. But, I know how to mine. Not so many people there."

"Maybe I will come and join you later," Pearl suggested.

"You come anytime you want," Joe offered. "I will be waiting for you. You ask for me in Globe. Someone will know where I am."

"I promise. If it does not work out for me here, I will come and find you," Pearl said. Joe continued on to Globe. Pearl stayed in Phoenix, but a surprise was on the way, soon to arrive but a month later.

One night Pearl was nearing the end of her singing in a hotel, where she found work in Phoenix, when she heard a man's voice call out to her from the crowd.

"Pearl. Come to see me after the show."

Pearl stopped and looked around at the crowd of men who were listening to her sing. She heard a voice that she thought she recognized. An expression of absolute horror appeared on her face when she spotted who it was. It was Frank. What was he doing there was her only thought. Pearl left the stage immediately and hurriedly walked to the rear door to leave. Suddenly a hand grabbed her arm spinning her completely around. It was Frank.

"Where do you think you are going, Sweetheart? I have come a long way to see you."

Pearl looked in silence straight into Frank's eyes. "How did you find me?" Pearl asked in obvious anger and shock.

"Your mother told me where I would find you," he informed her.

"Oh. That is right. I did write to her. What did you say to her? That I left you for no reason?" Pearl yelled back at him.

"Did you tell her about my broken nose? Did you tell her about all the times you hit me?"

"Please," Frank begged. "I have changed. I have come all the way here to prove it to you."

"Don't even bother to follow me. You had all the chances that you will ever get from me," Pearl warned Frank. "I have grown up a lot since you last saw me. You stay out of here or I will have the bouncers beat the shit out of you."

Pearl hurried back into the safety of the men who were inside the saloon waiting for her to return to the stage. She completed her show but was never to return. Before dawn the following morning, Pearl was on the first train out of Phoenix south to Tucson, Arizona, where she would transfer to a stagecoach for the rest of the trip to Globe where Joe Boot had told her he would be. She knew that he would not let Frank anywhere near her.

CHAPTER 21

AS SOON AS Pearl arrived in Globe she headed for the nearest saloon to see if anyone there would know where Joe might be found. She entered through the swinging doors and approached the bartender.

"Whiskey from the top shelf," Pearl requested.

"Yes, Lady, coming right up," he replied. "Haven't seen you around here before, new in town, are ya?"

"Ya. I am looking for Joe Boot. Ever heard tell of him?" Pearl asked.

The bartender poured Pearl a drink and handed it to her. Pearl grabbed the glass. She finished the drink in one swallow and handed the glass back for a refill.

"Hard telling," the bartender replied. "They come and go so much. He been in the area long?"

"Only a couple of months," Pearl said finishing her second drink.

"Most likely he be at the Old Dominion Mine a short distance from Globe. You could ask at the mercantile across the street," he suggested. "He likely does his business there."

"Thank you," Pearl said as she turned to look in the direction of the mercantile.

"The supply wagon is there now. I can see it from here. I know the driver would not mind giving a pretty thing like you a hitch to the mine" he suggested.

Pearl grabbed the bottle. "A silver dollar enough for the rest of the bottle?" she asked.

"Sure enough," he responded.

"Thank you, very much," Pearl yelled back as she hurried out of the saloon and ran towards the wagon. Pearl reached the wagon and looked around the area for the driver but could not spot him.

"What do ya need Miss?" the driver asked as he approached Pearl from the back of the full wagon.

"I was told that you might give me a ride to the Old Dominion Mine site," Pearl said.

"You know someone there?" the driver inquired.

"I be looking for Joe Boot," Pearl responded. "You know of him?"

"Yes, I know of him. Hard worker, no luck," he responded.

"He tried a claim that he purchased. No luck. No color. So he started working at the Old Dominion Mine. He is a good worker so he is still there. But, he spent everything he had on his claim. He is broke," the driver continued.

"Maybe I can help change his luck," Pearl suggested.

"Come on. I will take you to him," the driver offered as he jumped up into the seat and reached to offer Pearl his hand.

"Can you cook?" the driver asked.

"Of course I can cook," Pearl answered.

"Then there is a job up there for you. The Oriental man up there, he has a good cook wagon. But, he can't cook worth a donkey's shit," the driver said as he swished the reins to get the horses going.

"You ask for Yu. He won't pay much, but he will give you a place to stay and all the free food you and your friend can eat," the driver added.

"Oh. Thank you so much," Pearl yelled out over the wagon noise. "How can I ever thank you?"

"Just feed me good food when I deliver," he suggested.

"Oh. Yes I will," Pearl promised.

"Then I will give you a ride anytime," the driver offered.

It took about an hour and the wagon turned into the road to the mine that could be seen ahead.

"My name is Jack," he informed Pearl as the wagon slowed enough to be able to hear him speak. "You will find Yu in the cabin in back of the cook shack. He will not mind if you feed me. He feeds me when I bring him his supplies. But, you ask so he not get mad at you. What is your name pretty thing?"

"My name is Pearl," she answered.

Pearl stepped down off the wagon as it stopped and tipped her hat to the driver. She then walked to the cabin behind the cook wagon. Seeing no one, she walked back to the cook wagon and looked for Yu. No one there so she returned to the cabin.

"Hello in there," Pearl yelled as she stood by the door. "Mr. Yu. Are you in there?"

"I in here. What you want. You wait," a commanding Oriental voice could be heard from within the cabin.

"O.K. I will wait," Pearl responded.

As Pearl waited she wandered around the camp site. She looked over the cook wagon and the supplies. Looked to see where the water came from and noticed a water pump nearby.

"What you want?" the Oriental gentleman asked, startling Pearl from behind.

"I need a job. Jack, the driver, said that you need a cook," Pearl answered. "I am a good cook."

"Yes. I need a cook," he responded. "You eat free. I pay one dollar a day. That's all. No more."

"That is better than nothing," Pearl obliged.

"You start today. It is now three o'clock. The miners will start to come in two hours. Will be very hungry. You must make venison stew. You know how to make venison stew?" he asked.

"Yes. I know how to make venison stew," Pearl assured him. "I see Opuntia Cactus nearby. I can make a salad from the pads and flowers and make a Prickly Pear salad dressing for it," Pearl suggested.

"You make anything you want," Yu informed her, "as long as the miners like it."

"Do you know Joe Boot?" Pearl inquired.

"Yes. I know him. He should be here for dinner. But, he comes usually after dark. Maybe eight o'clock. I go to sleep now. Me tired. You need me, you wake me."

"O.K." Pearl responded.

Yu disappeared into his cabin. Pearl familiarized herself as to where everything was around the cook cart. What supplies there were to cook with and what there was to cook. She found that Yu had already prepared the venison stew so she needed only to heat it over the fire. She stoked the fire and added additional wood. She then collected the Opuntia and Prickley Pear cactus for the salad and found where Yu had some bread.

Pearl set up two barrows, filled them with beer, and covered them with ice from the nearby saloon. This was her idea and would be the first time that beer was sold outside of the saloon. Before this, the miners had to buy the beer at the saloon and then bring it with them.

By the time the first miner arrived, Pearl was standing by the pot of hot stew ready to serve them.

"Well, what do we have here?" the first miner said as he approached Pearl at the serving area of the cook cart. "You sure are a pleasing sight compared to old Yu. Bet you can cook better too."

"You will be very happy with what I cook for you," Pearl responded. My name is Pearl, how are you doing at the mine now?"

"Not very good," he answered with a tone of depression. "Color is hard to find now. If it does not hurry up and get better I am afraid some mines will start to close. The price of gold and silver is down. We are finding good copper but no demand now."

For the following three hours a steady flow of miners passed through the food line. Not a complaint could be heard. A lot of smiles could be seen. Pearl kept looking for Joe and was about to surprise him as he was now in line to be served.

"Here you are, sir" Pearl shyly offered the next in line.

"Holly shit. Pearl, is that you?"

"Yes. It is me," Pearl responded gleefully." Frank showed up in Phoenix so I left as soon as I could get on a train west. He lied and beat the Hell out of me twice. Never again will he do that to me."

"I am so glad to see you," Joe replied. "I hoped every day that you would show up. You can come to my cabin if you need a place to stay. It is not much, but it is a roof. I have not done as well as I thought I would. Silver is getting hard to find. Mostly copper. No money in copper now."

"Ya, that is what everybody has said," Pearl related. "I am O.K. here, for now. Yu lets me live in back of the cook shack for free."

"O.K., but if that changes, you let me know," Joe reassured Pearl.

Pearl's first day at the Old Dominion Mine had come to a close. It was a good day. She met a lot of miners, she found a job, and she found a place to lay her head in safety. She pulled the blanket up over herself and closed her eyes in anticipation of the days to come.

"Where are you little woman?" Yu's voice sharply awakened Pearl the following morning before there was even a sign of the morning sun. "Time to start breakfast, the miners will be here in an hour."

Pearl opened her eyes to discover that it had not even started to become light. Sitting up on her bed, which was but a thin mattress on the hard dirt floor, she could see the image of Yu walking towards her.

"Here is your coffee," Yu offered handing Pearl a full cup. "You need coffee. Tomorrow you get up yourself. You make the coffee."

"Thank you," Pearl said in appreciation as she reached for the cup. "I will be up to make the coffee tomorrow morning. I promise."

Several weeks passed without change. A welcomed event in Pearl's life. The miners arrived for their meals and by now Pearl had made friends with many of them.

"Good morning, Joe," Pearl greeted Joe as he arrived for breakfast. "Are things looking up yet?"

"No, they aren't" Joe responded sharply. "I will have to do something soon. I am just about out of money."

"I wish I could help" Pearl responded. "But, I received a letter from my brother asking for money to help my mother who has gotten very sick. I saved a little and sent it to him. I have nothing to help you with."

Joe announced, "I was thinking of maybe delivering supplies to the Old Dominion Mine from Globe. But, that won't last long either. You could do that with me. The way it is going a cook will not be needed here."

"I will think about it," Pearl answered.

It took about another week and Pearl could see that the camp would soon be shutting down. She saw Joe as he arrived in the camp and walked up to her.

"I have decided to leave and go with you," Pearl announced.

"I will come and get you during the night," Joe offered. "Yu will not know that you are gone until morning."

CHAPTER 22

IT WAS LONG before daybreak. But, Pearl was standing anxiously outside the shack waiting for the sound of Joe's wagon. As soon as she could hear it she would walk along the dark road and meet him so as not to awaken Yu.

Soon Pearl could hear the faint sound of the wagon. She stooped to pick up her bag containing her worldly belongings and began to walk in the direction of the wagon sounds as they grew a little louder. Joe stopped the wagon when he could see the shadow of Pearl walking towards him on the road in the bright light of a near full moon. Pearl approached the wagon and threw her bag in the back as she climbed up onto the seat next to Joe.

"Welcome aboard," Joe greeted Pearl. "I was afraid that you might change your mind."

"No chance," Pearl assured Joe. "I have cooked for enough miners. I was getting restless to move on."

"You are going to have to yell," Joe informed Pearl. "I cannot hear you very well over the noise of the wagon."

"How long will it take to get to Globe?" Pearl inquired.

"It will take all night and most of the day," Joe informed her.

"Do you know anyone there?"

"I have a friend at the Mammoth Silver Mine. He said that there is a claim next to his that we may be able work between supply trips."

"Is there at least a structure to live in?" Pearl asked.

"Yes. But not much of one," Joe answered. "There is a wood stove that will keep us warm. But, do not worry. I have another plan."

Late the following day Joe and Pearl arrived at the Ramboz mine camp not far from the Mammoth Silver Mine. Silver had run itself out and it was now a copper mine. Joe's friend, Henry Wagner, was one of the founders of the Old Dominion Mine but, left it when the silver ran out, hoping to find silver at the Ramboz, which had been abandoned.

"Henry, are you in there?" Joe announced their arrival.

"Ya, I am in here. Who wants to know?" a voice from inside inquired.

"Joe Boot."

After a short pause a man appeared at the door. Then he walked out to the wagon.

"Howdy, Joe", the man greeted them. "I am very surprised to see you. Never thought you would show up here. Who is the pretty thing with you?"

"Pearl. I met her in Phoenix," Joe replied.

"You are both certainly welcome," Henry assured them. "The building next to mine is empty. You can use it. Come back and we will talk after you settle in."

"O.K.," Joe accepted the offer. "I will be back in a few minutes."

"I will have some stew ready," Henry further offered.

Joe and Pearl unloaded their wagon and walked to the building next to Henry's. It was sparsely furnished but did have two beds, a table, chairs and wood stove. Once their few belongings were transferred to the shack, Joe returned to Henry's to talk. Pearl elected to stay behind.

"You know that you are welcome to stay," Henry opened the conversation. "But, there is nothing here anymore. Only copper that would take a big operation to mine."

"I know," Joe informed him. "I just needed a place to bring Pearl. I have a plan. We will be here only a couple of days."

"What are you going to do?" Henry inquired.

"I can't tell you," was Joe's only response.

The men continued to talk for a short time. Then Joe thought it was time to let Pearl in on his plan. He first informed her that there was nothing there for them.

"What the Hell are we to do?" Pearl expressed with anger. "I left in a way Yu would never let me come back. I trusted you. I sent all my savings to my brother."

"I have a plan," Joe responded. "We will rob the Globe to Florence stagecoach."

"You are crazy, aren't you," Pearl responded in disbelief.

"Listen," Joe began to explain, "I have given it a lot of thought. There used to be a lot of stage robberies around here. But, there have been none for a long time. The Globe to Florence runs through Cane Springs Canyon. I know the area very well. In the canyon there is a bend in the road where they come to a stop by the river to water the horses. We can surprise them and then disappear into the canyon. It would be a day before anyone would be looking for us. By then we could be well on our way to Tucson where we could take a train north to your mother's."

"You make it sound awful easy. What about the horses?" Pearl asked.

"I have two saddles in the back of the wagon," Joe informed Pearl. "You do know how to ride a horse, don't you?"

"Not really," she replied.

"I will lead your horse," Joe assured her. "You will just have to hold on."

"But, I am a girl."

"You don't have to look like one," Joe suggested.

"What about a gun?"

"I have a rifle and a shotgun," Joe replied.

That night Pearl began the transformation into looking as if she were a man. No one would suspect; cross dressing was not a common thing. Pearl cut her hair short enough with a knife so as to be able to tuck the rest under her hat. Nearby there was housing for the miners that were working the mine. Pearl went from one clothes line to another until she had acquired a complete man's outfit.

"You don't look like any girl to me," Joe commented as he saw Pearl in her new clothes.

The following morning Pearl and Joe left at the first ray of sunlight for their ride to Cane Springs Canyon, about a 30 mile ride southwest of Globe. By evening they reached their destination where the road crossed the Gila River. Joe knew that this was where the driver would stop for the water break.

"This is where we will be when the stagecoach arrives tomorrow," Joe began to explain to Pearl. "It should arrive here about ten in the morning. We will be on our way before noon. That will give us until evening before anyone can get to Florence. They will not be here to look for us until the next day."

"Let's pick out a place to bed down," Pearl suggested, beginning to sound the part she was playing. "We could use it to hide until they arrive."

Both Pearl and Joe dismounted and entered the thick underbrush that grew along the river to find a spot to hold out and wait.

"This looks like a good spot," Pearl suggested as she found a small opening in the brush. "We can hide here real easy and still see them when they arrive."

It had begun to become a realization as night fell. Morning would arrive all too soon. Pearl and Joe lay in their bedrolls in anticipation of the morning. Morning did arrive and there was only the wait in front of them. Time was getting short until the expected arrival. No sound of the coach could be heard.

"Listen hard," Joe said. "We should hear it any time now. Are you O.K.?"

"I am nervous," Pearl responded. "I am scared."

"Listen," Joe announced. "I can hear it coming."

The stagecoach could be heard as it came closer and closer, as if in slow motion, as the two lay in wait within the tall underbrush that surrounded them.

"Remember what to do," Joe cautioned. "Stay low and quiet. Watch for my signal to approach them."

Suddenly the stagecoach pulled up and stopped next to the river right where Joe had said it would. The driver could be heard giving instructions to the passengers to get out and stretch while he got the water for the horses. They could see that there were four passengers, the driver, and one brakeman. Only the brakeman had a gun that was visible and he left it at his seat in the couch when he stepped down.

"O.K. Pearl," Joe whispered. "It is time. I will come out as soon as you get their attention."

Pearl stepped out into the road and fired a shot into the air with her shotgun. She stood motionless with her shirt covering part of her face.

"Everyone stand where you are and face me," Pearl ordered in the deepest voice she could muster. "Put your hands in the air where I can see them and move closer together. Driver, drop your pistol on the ground in front of you and kick it to me."

Joe moved closer to where Pearl stood with both horses. All four passengers, the driver, and the brakeman, stood motionless in shock as fear began to consume their every thought as to what might happen next.

"I have a sack," Pearl further instructed. "I want each of you, one at a time, to come here to me and put your money in it."

Each of them came forward as instructed and emptied their pockets. They then stepped back slowly to the spot that they had left.

"Joe, reach up and get the driver's rifle" Pearl instructed as she appeared to enjoy what she was doing.

As Joe was getting the brakeman's rifle, Pearl went to each person and handed them a $1 bill. She then walked backward to her horse that Joe had the reins to and climbed into the saddle.

"You each now have a dollar," Pearl spoke to the victims. "I did that so you can eat when you get to town. Sorry that we had to do this to you. We will go now."

Pearl and Joe then entered the river, which was low, and rode east towards the San Pedro River. Once they reached the San Pedro River they would follow it south towards Benson. They stopped north of Benson to bed down for the night.

"This should be a safe spot to get some rest until daybreak," Joe suggested as he pulled his horse to a stop. "They won't come after us until daylight and that should give us plenty of time to be well on our way to Tucson for the train to Colorado. How much money did we get?"

"Not very much," Pearl answered. "I got $380 off a salesman, a 'tenderfoot' had $35, and the Chinaman had $5. I did get a watch from the salesman."

"We had better bed down and get some rest," Joe suggested.

Meanwhile Henry Beacon, the stagecoach driver, did one thing that Joe had not thought of. He unhitched one of the horses and set out immediately for Globe to report the holdup to Sheriff W.T. Armstrong. The posse went into action immediately, rather than wait until dawn, as Joe had thought they would. Also, a telegram was sent to Benson alerting the sheriff there, who also sent out a posse towards Globe. Within five hours of when Pearl and Joe had bedded down to sleep, the posse from Benson was following the San Pedro River Road when they noticed the smell of a smoldering campfire. Dismounting, they slowly, quietly, approached the area of the smoke. They circled the spot where Joe and Pearl were sleeping. They pulled their pistols and fired several rounds in the air. It meant the end of a grand total of fifteen hours of freedom following the robbery, due to the oversights of an inexperienced robber.

Awakened by the yelling and gunfire, Joe and Pearl sprang

to their feet and grabbed their guns. But, they found themselves looking straight into the mouths of two gaping Winchesters in the hands of the sheriff and his posse.

"Resistance will be your worse move," the sheriff warned. "I suggest that you put those guns down right now."

Both Pearl and Joe slowly lay their guns on the ground as instructed.

"Turn around so that I can tie your hands," he instructed.

"Yes sir," they responded in unison.

Both turned around with a glaring eye contact with each other and placed their hands crossed together at their wrist. They stood motionless in silence.

"Now, get on your horses," he ordered. "We are taking you to the Florence jail."

Joe and Pearl were taken to Florence for a preliminary hearing and held without bail until they could go before the grand jury. The local jail had no provisions for a female prisoner, so Pearl was transferred to the Pima County jail in Tucson immediately the following morning.

CHAPTER 23

"THIS WILL BE your cell," the jail attendant informed Pearl at the Pima County jail. "There is a man in a cell in the next room. Don't worry about him. He is not dangerous but, he may come in here to say hello to ya. He is in and out of here from time to time to sober up. We don't lock his cell so he can walk out when he wakes up. If he does bother you, let me know and we will lock him in. His name is Ed Hogan. Are you O.K. with that?"

"Yes sir," Pearl answered. "That will be fine. I would like someone to talk to anyway."

"He will certainly take care of that for you," the attendant assured her. You get some sleep. Yell if you need anything. We will bring you food in the morning."

"Thank you sir," Pearl quietly answered.

For the following three months Pearl and Ed got to know each other quite well during his several visits to the jail. He would spend much of the time visiting Pearl's cell after sobering up before he left the jail in the morning, knowing he would be back soon.

"You know, Ed," Pearl said as she was talking to him on one of his visits while sitting on the floor next to her cell door, "you seem to be able to get around at will around here."

"Ya, they pretty much just bring me in to sober up and let me leave when I wake up," he responded. "They have nobody on duty at night and leave the back door unlocked for me so I can leave any time."

"If you help me get out of here I will do anything you want me to do," Pearl offered. "I will take you with me. You can have me your way."

"Where would we go?" Ed asked.

"Anywhere but here," Pearl answered. "You have no reason to stay here. But, I am a reason for you not to. We could go to New Mexico."

"It would be easy," Ed admitted. "The wall to the cell is only a lath and plaster partition. We could cut a hole in the wall easily with a knife and fork that they bring you for your dinner. Keep a knife from one meal and a fork from the next. They would never notice."

That night, Ed entered the rear room of the county record office on the second floor that was directly under Pearl's cell. From there he entered an adjoining small room that contained a stairwell that led to the tower of the building. There was a door from a small room on the second floor to the courthouse. Ed entered the courthouse, walked up the stairs and entered the room adjoining Pearl's cell. It took but a few minutes for Ed to cut a small hole through the wall of her cell.

"Come on Pearl," Ed urged. "Take my hand and I will pull you through."

Pearl reached through the hole and after a few tries he successfully pulled her through. Holding her hand, he led her down the flight of stairs and out the door to the street. With no night watchman on duty, they had no worry of being caught.

"Come on," Ed instructed, "follow me. I have two horses tied up with enough provisions to get us across the border and into New Mexico."

Pearl and Ed made their way east over the next three days, stopping in Lordsburg, New Mexico, where they figured it would be safe, thus adding another chapter to Pearl's remarkable trail of events.

The moment they entered the border town of Lordsburg, New Mexico, the main priority was to enter the first saloon that they could find. Ed had provided a bottle or two in their provisions, but, that was likely celebrated away long before they crossed the border.

"Let's hit the saloon," Ed strongly suggested as he spotted one on the edge of town.

"A whiskey sounds good to me too," Pearl agreed. "If we run out of money I can sing for more."

Pearl had a chance to learn from the novice mistakes that led to her and Joe's fast arrest after the robbery. But, it seems she did not pay attention. When you escape with a known drunk the most likely place to head is the border, and the first saloon across the border would seem to be a likely place to stay away from.

However, for the next three days Pearl and Ed spent all of their waking hours drinking at the first bar near Lordsburg. Pearl did what she did best and sang when they needed money. She did very well pulling in enough to support their fun. As the money ran out and the crowds pulled away, they moved on to the next town, East Deming, and started over. But, due to their guard being totally absent, their luck was soon to run out. Sitting at a table by himself, in a corner of the saloon where Pearl was singing, was a man listening and reading the latest edition of the Cosmopolitan magazine. Suddenly, he recognized a picture of Pearl in an article about her escape and the stagecoach robbery. The man happened to be George Scarsborough, a U.S. Marshal from Deming.

U.S. Marshal Scarsborough slowly made his way towards the stage where Pearl was singing to the music of a piano player. Out of uniform, Pearl thought he was coming to give her money. But, to her surprise, he grabbed her arm and pulled her from the stage and dragged her outside the saloon.

"Thought that you were safe, didn't you?" the marshal proudly barked at Pearl.

"What are you doing," Pearl exclaimed. "I didn't do anything."

"I am a U.S. Marshal and I know who you are. You will be on

the train back to Tucson in the morning. Come with me without a fight and I won't put the handcuffs on you. We are going to walk across the street to the jail. There will be a train going through in the morning to return you to Tucson."

"What happened to Ed?" Pearl asked as they were walking across the street.

"I have no idea where he is," he responded. "Right now, I could give a damn. I have you."

The Marshal led Pearl handcuff free across the street to the jail where she would remain until the following morning and the arrival of the next train west to Tucson. Word traveled fast and the following morning nearly the whole town turned out to see Pearl as she was led in handcuffs to the train. No attention was ever given to Ed Hogan and his whereabouts was never known. Pearl had become a sort of legend throughout the territory. Sheriff W.T. Armstrong was waiting on the station platform when the train arrived in Tucson.

"You will not escape me or the Pima County jail again, I promise you," he warned Pearl as he took over her guard. "Where you were before was for your comfort. This time, you will be in the same jail as everyone else. Your cell will be private because you are a female. That is the only special treatment that you will receive while you are here."

"How long will I be there?" Pearl inquired.

"Likely three to four weeks." he responded. "Why are you shaking so much?" the sheriff inquired. "What are you on?"

"I am on opium," Pearl responded.

"When did that start?"

"First when I started to cook for Yu at the mining camp," Pearl replied. "He had it all the time. I was also able to get some in Lordsburg."

"We will have to keep an eye on you," he assured her. "But, you will get none of that here."

Pearl ended up staying in Tucson only one week as her court date was moved up and she was transferred to Florence to stand trial.

"Come on Pearl," a court attendant announced. "It is time for your day in court."

"I signed a paper admitting that I did all those things. Why do I still have to go to court?" Pearl questioned.

"Because you have to tell the judge, and the jury has to read the evidence and your admittance and agree upon a decision of what to do with you," the Court Deputy informed her. "Come on. We must go."

As she was led into the courtroom all heads turned as she came through the door. The sheriff led Pearl through the doors at the back of the courthouse and directly to a spot in front of the judge.

"I am Judge Long," he introduced himself. In front of us is Pearl Hart. She has admitted her guilt to the armed robbery of a stage-coach. Has the jury read the admittance and evidence and come to a decision?" the judge asked.

"Yes, your Honor, we have," the Jury Chairman announced. "We, the jury, have accepted it as read."

"How does the jury find the defendant?" the judge demanded.

"We believe that she acted under duress because of needing the money for her ailing mother, and, we believe, she being of a naïve nature and heavily influenced by another, a Joe Boot, find the defendant not guilty 11 to 1 of armed robbery."

"How the Hell can you find her not guilty when she admitted to doing it?" the judge exclaimed with a great deal of anger. "I am not to be swayed by her prettiness, or her smile. I am not going to be swayed by pity and let her free. Marshal, arrest Pearl Hart for the crime of robbery of the stagecoach driver's gun. I find her guilty of a lesser crime, as I have the privilege of doing, and sentence her immediately to spend 5 years in the Yuma Territorial Prison in Yuma, Arizona."

"But Judge," you can't do that without putting it to the jury," the District Attorney objected.

"Try me," the judge challenged. "I can charge anyone for a lessor crime and sentence immediately. Court is now adjourned."

CHAPTER **24**

Yuma Territorial Prison, November, 17ᵗʰ, 1899

PEARL WAS TRANSFERRED and arrived at the Yuma Territorial Prison on November 17ᵗʰ, 1899. She was delivered to the prison by a prison wagon that appeared to be a prison cell on the back of a buck wagon. It was open so all could see the now infamous Pearl Hart as she arrived. News of her arrival preceded her and at least 200 people were waiting for their chance to see the now called "Bandit Queen" as the wagon rolled past and through the open outer steel door of the prison. The steel door closed as quickly as it opened as soon as the wagon cleared the entrance.

"Come on little girl, this is going to be your home for a long time," a guard said as he gently took hold of her arm and led her.

Pearl was taken directly to a small room for processing.

"You sit here," the guard instructed her. "A woman guard will come in a few minutes and do a strip search and then she will give you prison clothes."

Pearl just sat in silence. Fear was obvious on her face as she wiped an occasional tear from her cheek.

The guard then left the room leaving Pearl alone handcuffed to a chair. Pearl continued to sit silently as she panned the room continually with her teary eyes. Suddenly the door opened and a female prison nurse and a female guard entered. The female guard just moved to a corner of the room and stood in silence.

"Stand up and I will take the handcuffs off." The nurse instructed Pearl. "Now take all of your clothes off. I must search you for drugs and anything that you could make a weapon out of."

The nurse performed the body search.

"You could at least try to make it look like you don't enjoy do-ing that, you know," Pearl said sarcastically.

The nurse ignored her.

"Follow me," the nurse ordered. "You will next get washed down." The nurse led Pearl through a door and into a windowless shower room and washed Pearl down with a fire hose. By now the fear had overcome Pearl and she began to cry loudly. Showing no sympathy, the nurse instructed her to towel dry herself and to put on the prison clothes that she provided her. As soon as Pearl was dressed the nurse led her to another larger room which had one small window. The first window Pearl had seen since arriving. The nurse instructed Pearl to sit in a chair near the center of the room and proceeded to handcuff Pearl to it.

"This is the process room," the nurse began to explain. "You will be admitted here. A man will be coming in and he will be asking a lot of questions. You must answer each and every question and answer honestly. You do not want to start off wrong in this room."

Again Pearl was left alone with only her thoughts. It was but a few moments and the door reopened and two men entered. One of the men had a guard's uniform on and the other was dressed in a black suit and tie. The guard said nothing. He just walked to a corner and stood in silence. The man in the suit walked to a desk that was near Pearl and sat down on the far side and looked at her.

"I am the Warden. You will not be treated special by me or any of the guards in any way," he warned Pearl. "This is a prison. Here, put this around your neck" he ordered as he handed Pearl a 6 inch round metal disc marked with the numbers 1559 in large numbers. Pearl put it over her head and it hung around her neck by a wire allowing it to fall to hang at chest level.

The warden stood up and approached Pearl. "I will now take the handcuffs off. They will stay off as long as you do and say what you are told. As soon as I get these off you I want you to stand against the wall so the guard can take your admittance picture."

Pearl slowly stood up. Her legs quivering, she walked as instructed in silence to the indicated wall and turned around. The guard took several pictures.

"Why so many pictures, are you going to sell them?" Pearl spoke out.

"This is the only nice warning that you are going to get," the guard warned Pearl. "You say nothing until this process is done."

"Yes sir. I am sorry."

"You can sit back down now," the guard instructed.

Pearl returned to her seat. The guard returned to his place against the wall. The warden sat in silence, shuffling through several papers.

"When you refer to me you say Warden, sir."

"Yes. Warden, sir," Pearl replied as instructed.

"I am going to read off several things," the warden continued. "Some describe you, and who you are. Some are about what you did and where. Do not interrupt me unless you hear me say something that is wrong."

"Yes, sir."

"What did you call me?"

"Yes Warden, sir. Sorry."

"Your name is Pearl Hart. Your number here is 1559. Do you have an alias?"

"No Warden, sir. Except I used Pete when I wanted to look like a boy when robbing the stagecoach."

"You use only Pearl Hart here."

"Yes Warden, sir."

"Your sentence is 5 years for robbery in Pinal County."

"Nativity: Canada. Age: 28. Legitimate occupation: none."

"Habits: Intemperate."

"You have taken opium, morphine, and smoke tobacco."

"Is there anything else that we should know? If so, say so now."

"No Warden, sir."

"Your height is five feet three inches and you weigh 100 pounds."

"Shoe size is 2-1/2."

"Color of hair black, eyes gray."

"You were with two children. You can read. You can write."

"No formal imprisonment until now."

"You were educated in the United States."

"Your nearest relative is your mother, Mrs. James Taylor, Jr."

"Would there be anything else that I should know?"

"No Warden, sir." Pearl responded.

"We are done here, for now," the warden continued. "Thank you Pearl for your behavior. Please keep it that way. The guard will now take you to your quarters. He will explain some of the reasons for discipline and what types of discipline you could get if you do not follow the rules."

The warden stood and left the room.

"Come on Pearl," the guard instructed. "Follow me."

The guard, seeing the fear in Pearl's eyes, reached for her hand. Pearl slowly reached for his hand and accepted his help as she stood up and followed him to the door. Before going through the door, the guard took off her handcuffs. "I am not really allowed to take those off. But, I know that you will behave yourself. Won't you?"

"I will behave myself," Pearl assured him.

As they walked through the door Pearl could see a narrow, long, and roofless alley with a wall and several barred openings on both sides. Looking straight ahead to the far end was another barred opening leading to an outside courtyard.

"These are the cells for the general population," the guard explained. "You will not be staying in these. You are the only and the first female that has been incarcerated here so you will be staying in this cell by yourself," the guard explained.

"I know that there are other women prisoners here. Why are you lying to me?" Pearl questioned.

"I must say what I am told to say. Beyond that, there is so much publicity about you that I am to take you to the southwest corner of the prison where there is a cell carved into the sandstone cliff that is as large as an ordinary bedroom."

"I asked for no special treatment," Pearl assured the guard. "I even admitted my guilt."

"I have no say in that. I do know that it is excavated into the hillside and that you have a "house yard" in which to do your constitution and whatever else is needed for you women."

The guard unlocked the cell door. Pearl walked in, turned around and watched the door as it slammed shut. She then walked to the bed and sat on its edge. For the first time in many years she broke down into an uncontrollable cry.

On Joe Boot's sentencing he also went to the same Territorial Prison and was sentenced to 30 years. He did not stay long, however. He became a model prisoner leading to becoming a trustee. On February 6th, 1901, he escaped and disappeared in Mexico, after serving only two years.

A guard approached Pearl's cell. She had been in prison for nearly 3 years. She was desperate to get out now. She had a plan but needed her sister in Kansas to make it work.

"You have a visitor waiting for you," the guard announced. "Please follow me."

Pearl followed the guard to the visiting area where her sister and husband were waiting. Following a greeting of hugs the three sat at a table in the courtyard. Pearl had asked her sister to come.

"Thank you for coming. I have a plan to get out of here and I need to show the Warden that I do have family out there to make sure it will work. If he knows I have a place to go, with my plan, I know he will pardon me."

"As long as you do it legal, of course you may come to our house" her sister Mrs. Frizzle responded.

"I will tell them that I want to play my own part about the robbery," Pearl responded.

"You are an actress. They will believe you," her sister said.

Her sister had agreed to help Pearl with that part of her plan. She was not told the full story. But, this gave Pearl the assurance she needed. She really had thought to draw upon her inspiration from Annie Oakley and try to join the Wild Bill Show. For that reason Pearl was not totally using her sister. Pearl waited a few weeks and then started the rest of her plan.

"Guard, I need to see the Warden," Pearl yelled out at a passing guard in the yard.

"I will let him know," he responded.

Within a few hours Pearl was sitting in the Warden's office nervously awaiting his arrival. Finally the door opened.

"What is it that you wanted to see me about?" he asked as he sat at his desk.

"I have a serious problem, sir," Pearl began. "I was not sure but, I am two months late for my woman's time and I never am. I must be pregnant."

The Warden just stared at Pearl in disbelief of what he had heard. His concern was not necessarily because it was he that the finger would be pointed at, but, that it did not matter who. No one could possibly have been with Pearl to cause this but himself, one of two guards, a priest, and the Governor of Arizona, Governor Brodie. Governor Brodie was known to be a man of desires. No matter who or how, this would not look good for him or the prison.

Several hastily arranged meetings were held between the worried parties. All, of course, had denied any possible sexual contact with Pearl. The problem is this: could any of them take the chance of being blamed? Suspicion was heightened due to two visits to Pearl by the Governor soon after the announcement.

Within a few days a guard approached Pearl's cell. "Come on, Pearl. The Warden has asked me to bring you to his office." He opened the door and Pearl followed the guard directly to the Warden's office. Opening the office door, she could see him sitting at his desk waiting for her.

"You wanted to see me, sir?" Pearl announced her arrival.

"Yes. Please sit."

"I have no way to know if what you say about being pregnant is true without waiting until you start showing it. I cannot take that chance. This is either a bad mistake on someone's part or the slickest plan I have ever heard of. In any event, you have given me no choice. On this day, December the 2nd, 1902, I have been ordered by Governor Brodie of Arizona Territory, to let you go. He has issued an Order of Pardon."

Pearl sat in silence, not sure that she believed what he had just told her.

"There is one condition," the Warden continued. "He has sent with the letter to pardon you a one way train ticket to Kansas City. You are to be on the train. You also may not return to Arizona before the date your sentence expires. That would be November 17th, 1904. Do you agree with and fully understand the conditions of you pardon?"

"Oh, yes sir," Pearl replied as she began to realize what was really happening.

"Then return to your cell," he further instructed, "and you have six hours to be ready to leave. The next train arrives this evening for Kansas City and you must be on it. A guard will come and get you and escort you to the station."

Pearl excitedly ran back to her cell, rolled her personals into a blanket, then sat and waited very impatiently for the guard to come and get her. In the few hours until the train was to arrive, the news traveled very fast that the "Bandit Queen" had been pardoned and that she would be on the train to Kansas City. Many people and reporters, including one from the Cosmopolitan magazine, were beginning to arrive at the train station in anticipation of Pearl's arrival.

Pearl soon arrived to a cheering crowd that had grown to spill beyond the station platform. The train had arrived and was taking on water and supplies.

"Come on people," the guard requested showing his irritation. "Move aside and let us through."

"Pearl, stop trying to please the people and get on the train," the guard ordered.

The guard pushed Pearl up the train stairs and waited until she disappeared within the confines of the train. He stepped back and walked along the outside of the train and watched Pearl until she found a seat. He then stepped back and watched with the crowd to make sure Pearl remained on the train. As the train began to pull out of the station the crowd started to wave and yell their goodbye to one of the most colorful prisoners to have ever been incarcerated in the Yuma Territorial Prison.

As the train pulled into Kansas City Pearl looked out the window in an attempt to see her sister. She finally spotted her and waved joyfully.

"Thank you for helping me to get out of that place," Pearl said excitedly as she ran up to her sister.

"I only hope that they never realize what a trick you played on them," her sister replied.

"I don't think that they will really ever care as long as I don't ever come back," Pearl replied assuredly.

"What are you going to do, now?" her sister question Pearl.

"What we did gave me an idea. I'm still thinking that I might try to join Buffalo Bill's Wild West Show. I saw it in Chicago back in '93."

"I am afraid that that will not work," her sister announced. "The show left for Europe a few months ago. I was thinking that

that might work for you, too."

"I will find something," Pearl promised. "In two years I can go back to Arizona."

"I do have an idea, I know of a man who needs someone to run his cigar store."

"I can do that," Pearl responded.

"Come on, I will take you there."

Pearl hated the cigar store. But, she stayed on for almost the two years she had to wait to return to Arizona and finally finish her journey back to Globe. She had heard of a new hotel that had opened in the now busy town of Beatty, Nevada, near the California border. She could see no reason why she couldn't go there and work for the rest of the time.

"May I talk to the manager?" Pearl asked as she approached the desk of the New Montgomery Hotel in Beatty, Nevada.

"Just a moment, please. I will get him for you," the clerk obliged.

"That was impressive," Pearl thought to herself remembering how they usually say he is not available.

"How may I help you?" asked a gentleman formally dressed right down to the fancy cowboy boots.

"I am looking for work," Pearl responded.

"How can I say no to a cute little thing like you?" he answered. "Come back tonight and I will see how you do on the stage."

"Yes sir, and I do need a room," Pearl replied.

"I will have a room ready for you without charge for tonight," he offered. "If you like, the room is yours for as long as you work here."

"You can do that?"

"Sure. I own the place. My name is Ernest Montgomery. You may call me Mr. Bob."

"Oh. Thank you very much. You will like me," Pearl assured him.

"They are a rough crowd of miners at times," he warned her.

"I can handle them. I have before," Pearl answered.

The sound of a few hands clapping greeted Pearl her first night. She sang for an hour to the reluctant crowd before it began to warm up to her. Before the evening ended they were standing and cheering. By the end of the week she was packing the house.

She liked it in Beatty and the attention that she was receiving. So much so, two years passed before she began to get restless again. It was now September, 1906. Pearl decided it was time to complete her journey and boarded the Tonopah & Las Vegas Railroad train to Las Vegas where she would transfer to a Wells Fargo Stagecoach to Ivanpah, California. She could then connect to Phoenix, Arizona.

CHAPTER 25

PEARL SLYLY LOOKED up to Earl as she finished her story.

"That is O.K.," Earl assured her. "That is all past to you now. Come on," Earl said as he offered his hand, "Let's go back to the hotel and have a couple of drinks."

Pearl accepted Earl's hand. Their eyes meet in a silent stare. Their lips met in a passionate kiss. Pearl placed Earl's arm around her waist and they walked to the hotel.

The mood had been set and continued through three rounds of drinks. A fourth was ordered which they carried to a room they shared for the night.

The following morning, Earl dressed and left the room quietly so as not to awaken Pearl and walked to the rail depot to talk with Ralph, the attendant, about his first move towards his search for the underground river. He had to first find out where Kokoweef Mountain was. The name was given to him but the location of the mountain was not. He also wanted information about ranch property and if there may be a small business in town for sale or where Pearl may find work. He had not talked to her about it, but, when she showed interest in staying in Nipton, at least for a while, he wanted to do all he could to make that possible.

He had become quite fond of her which was most out of character for him.

"Ralph, do you have a moment to talk?" Earl asked as he approached him standing behind a large desk covered with papers in a manner of complete disarray.

"Sure. Want a coffee?"

"Please," Earl responded.

"Here," Ralph offered as he handed Earl a cup of coffee. "Sit" he instructed as they approached a small table across the room from the desk.

"What can I do for you?" the depot attendant offered.

"I am looking for Kokoweef Mountain. Could you tell me where it is?"

"From here it is about 5 miles a few degrees south of due west," he began to give Earl directions. "But, if you are planning on climbing the mountain or going to the peak, the last couple of miles are very steep and irregular. There are no roads and few paths."

"My suggestion," he continued, "would be to follow the tracks south then southwest until you reach Cima. That also is 5 miles. Then north three miles. It is longer. But much easier. A car or truck can make it all but the final climb if you plan to climb the peak."

"I don't have a vehicle yet. But, my brother and father will be arriving in a few days by train," Earl informed him. "They will have a truck with them."

"When you get to Cima, there is a water station there for the train before it must climb the Ivanpah Mountain Range," Ralph continued. "Dave is the attendant there and I will send a message for him to expect you and to be of assistance. You may also find it a handy place for you to keep supplies if you plan to be out there for a few days. You could rent one of the bachelor cabins he has there. They are small and only one room. But, they have a bed, stove, outhouse, and you could cook."

"That sounds like what I will need," Earl commented.

"He does have supplies there you can buy," Ralph further informed him. "He supplies the miners in the area. There are many. He cooks. And serves whiskey."

"I would have a gun with you," he warned. "They are very nervous about claim jumpers out there. You must be careful. Also, there is known to be a few Indians out there that are not very

friendly if you get too close to where they live. It is not very friendly out there if they don't know you."

"Do you know of a ranch that may be available for cattle?" Earl
asked as he went on to the next question.

"There is an abandoned ranch that is livable in open range
land in the New York Mountains about thirty miles to the north
from here. I know there is a well there also," Ralph suggested. "No
one will bother you there. The miner that lived there died a few
months ago. Been empty since."

"Anything else?" Ralph inquired.

"Well. There is one more thing. Is there some work or something I could buy for the girl to run that came in with me?"

"How long do you plan to stay here?" he asked Earl.

"I will be likely staying in the area for several years if my plans
work out and I want to make it appealing for her to stay with me,"
Earl responded with a gesture with his hands reaching upward.

"My immediate thought could be the hotel you are staying in,"
Ralph suggested after giving it some thought.

"It is not totally for sale," he continued. "But, the owner,
Samuel Karns is looking for someone to be operating owner. That
might work."

"Shit. That might work," Earl spoke with excitement. "I have
the money and, believe me, she has the experience. Can you tell
me some more about him?"

"He came here as a gold seeker from western Pennsylvania
before the turn of the century," the man began to explain. "He was
attracted to the activity in the Vanderbilt Gold District just up the
Ivanpah Valley from what was the crossroads that formed Nippeno,
what we now call Nipton. On January 1, 1900, he and some associates staked the earliest claim in the Crescent District, to be
given the name Nippeno, later to be followed by adjacent claims
Susquehana, Cumberland, North Cumberland, Pennsylvania, and
Osceola. Together to be named the Nippeno Consolidated Mine.

The camp with it, Nippeno Camp. He does not want to get rid of the hotel completely, but, he has no time to run it anymore."

"Do you know how much he wants for a working partner?" Earl further inquired.

"I believe all he wants is $10,000 while retaining half interest," Ralph informed him.

"I am interested. How do I meet him?"

He will be at the hotel very soon. He eats there every morning when in town," Ralph informed Earl. "He is in town today. You are very lucky."

"Thank you for all your help," Earl thanked him as he rose from the table hurriedly. "I will let you know."

"Good luck. When I see him I will tell him you are a good man," he offered.

Earl left the depot and headed directly for the hotel not wanting to miss his chance to meet this Mr. Karns. After listening to the story that Pearl had told him the night before, there was no question in his mind that, if she wanted to, she could very easily run the hotel and make a lot of outstanding changes. It would give him a place to return to from the mountains. It also would possibly keep Pearl in Nipton.

CHAPTER 26

EARL LEFT THE depot and returned to the hotel directly to locate this Mr. Karns.

"Has Mr. Karns arrived this morning?" Earl inquired as he approached a man behind the desk in the hotel lobby.

"Yes," the man responded acting slightly irritated. "That is him sitting by the window." He directed Earl nodding his head in the direction of a gruff looking middle age man alone by the corner table facing the street window.

"Thank you," Earl thanked the man with a nod.

"Careful," he warned. "He is not one to interrupt uninvited."

Without responding to his last comment, Earl tipped his hat in thanks and turned to go to the table where Mr. Karns was sitting.

"Excuse me, sir," Earl spoke carefully as he approached the man's table.

Slowly the man looked up from the paper he was reading and looked directly at Dorr in silence.

"What the Hell do you want?" the man finally spoke in a sharp tone.

"I was told by Ralph at the depot that you are looking for someone to purchase the operating interest of the hotel."

"That may be true," he responded. "What be your interest?"

"I have $10,000 that I will give you for half ownership and be responsible for operation of it," Earl quickly offered.

"Good. I have more important things to do," he responded with a demanding tone.

"You go to the Wells Fargo Bank down the street. They will give you the papers to sign. When the money is transferred into my account start running it," he said directly.

"Now, let me eat." He then returned to his meal and paper.

Without a word Earl turned to leave the room.

"Thank you," Earl heard the man say. "I will be back in town in two weeks. We will plan to sit and talk then."

Earl tipped his hat in acknowledgment and went to the bank to do as he had been directed. The town had awakened by now as Earl walked to the bank. Taking more notice now that he was about to become a businessman in Nipton, he was surprised as he noticed many empty buildings and the extreme lack of women in the town. Nipton was primarily a mining town. The people that followed the mining population were not the type of people he was used to in Colorado Springs. Here they were mostly dirty drunks looking for trouble. The few women were of questionable occupation. If he had not heard Pearl tell her story he would have worried much more than he did. It sounded like she knew how to handle the atmosphere in Nipton.

The bank was small and doubled as the post office. It consisted of a small room as you enter. Directly ahead was a wooden partitioned wall with one opening covered with heavy black rod iron bars. In the lower center was a small opening about one foot wide and three inches high. It took but a few minutes to complete what Earl had come to do. The small man behind the bars, complete with visor, hat, round glasses, white shirt and black bow tie, knew exactly what Earl wanted as soon as he mentioned the hotel and the money transfer.

Soon Earl found himself returning to the hotel he now owned half of, anxious to tell Pearl in hopes that she would agree to his planned offer.

"Good morning," Earl announced softly as he entered the room.

To his surprise, there was no response. Looking about he discovered that Pearl was not anywhere to be found. He then turned and left the room and returned to the hotel lobby where he could see Pearl sitting at the same window where he had been talking to Samuel Karns earlier.

"Good morning, Pearl," Earl announced himself as he approached the table.

"Good morning," Pearl responded as she looked up to Earl with a bright smile about her face. "Have a seat."

"I have an offer that I hope you will like," Earl opened the conversation cautiously. "No need to worry. If you are not interested I needed to do what I did anyway with my family arriving. I bought half of the hotel and would like you to run it for me. I know you can. You have done all aspects of running one before," he assured her. This came as a great surprise to the unsuspecting Pearl. With wide eyes, she stared back at Earl for what seemed a very long time before speaking.

"I know that I am capable of running this place and adding a lot of positive changes. I am just in shock." Pearl finally spoke with great pause between some of the words.

"I know that you can or I would not offer," Earl tried to encourage her.

"I cannot be tied to it. But I need it," he started to explain.

"I need a permanent connection with the town and a place to stay. But, I must be free to pursue what I came here for," Earl continued as Pearl listened very intently. "It also will provide a cash flow. I am not hurting. But, I am not stupid either. I must have a source of money to support what I want to do. It could be very expensive."

"When will you be leaving?" Pearl interrupted.

"I plan to leave for a short period in a day or two," Earl explained. "But, only for a few days. I must travel into the Ivanpah Mountains to see how far I must go and what it will entail."

"Can I have until you come back to decide?" Pearl inquired. "I would like to see what the town is like and talk to the employees.

To have a chance to think."

"Of course you can," Earl assured her. "I worry some because it looks like a rough town."

"I am used to that," Pearl reassured Earl. "I am well able to take care of myself. No asshole will bother me more than once."

Earl laughed and reached for Pearl's hand. "I hope you will stay," he nearly pleaded as he kissed her hand. "I will take very good care of you. I am not like those you told me about."

"I would hope not. I wouldn't want to have to kill you," Pearl warned him sternly.

"My brother and father will likely arrive while I am gone," Earl announced. "They are in transit. Just put them up and introduce yourself. I have told them of you. Not about you. They will need the bank and will need to be introduced properly to Ralph at the depot. He knows they are coming and will assist them."

"No promise. But, I think I may give it a try," Pearl softly spoke to Earl as she could see the concern in his facial expression. With raised eyebrows and a tight lip Earl returned a look of hope that reflected his true inner feelings. Something that he normally hid well.

"I must go to the mercantile and get supplies and then to the livery to acquire a horse and saddle. Would you like to join me?" Earl offered.

"Certainly," Pearl responded as she rose from the table.

"Charge that to my room," Earl instructed the waiter.

It had not been announced that he had bought into the hotel. Therefore nothing was said about it. Earl thought he and Pearl would announce the news together to the employees after she decided what she was going to do. Earl also wanted to get to know some of the people in the town but was avoiding that task until he knew what was to transpire. He figured she would tell him within a few hours so that they could make some plans after that. But, he wanted to start spreading the news before he left for the mountains.

"Good morning," a lady's voice greeted Earl and Pearl as they entered the mercantile. "How may I help you?" she offered.

"My name is Earl Dorr and this is Pearl," introducing themselves in a way to make it appear as husband and wife. "I need some supplies for a few days in the hills and I would like to open an account so Ms. Pearl can purchase while I am out of town."

"My name is Linda. My husband James is out right now. We would be glad to open an account for you," she offered as she opened a ledger and entered their names. "Where are you staying?" she inquired.

"At the Nipton Hotel," Earl informed her. "I realize I must give you some information for the account. Please allow me to tell others on my own time. We have purchased half ownership of the hotel and will be needing supplies and only you know at this time."

"Well. Welcome to Nipton," Linda responded gracefully. "I will not make it known about town. I will leave that to you."

"Thank you," Earl said as he reached to shake her hand.

"We also own the livery," she announced. "Would you be needing a horse and saddle for your trip?"

"Oh. Yes, Could that be put on the account also?"

"That will be fine," Linda agreed. "You could just rent the horse and saddle unless you would rather buy it," she suggested.

"Oh. That would be much better, thank you," Earl responded.

By midafternoon Earl and Pearl returned to the hotel with all supplies and needed arrangements completed for the days that Earl would be gone so that Pearl would be taken care of in his absence.

"How about a couple of whiskeys," Earl suggested as they entered the hotel.

"Yes," Pearl agreed.

As they sat at one of the tables on the bar side of the room, Pearl picked up her glass and looked Earl straight in the eye.

"I would be happy to stay and give it a try," she announced to Earl's pleasure.

"I am so glad," Earl responded gleefully thrusting his head backward then resting his head within his arms. "I want so much to give our relationship a chance. I never expected to find someone such as you and don't want to let you go."

"I have no reason to go now," she responded reassuringly. "I have been lost in life for so long with no direction. It is time to give it a chance. I am lucky to have found you. I would be stupid to run from you now."

So the plans had been set. They announced to the employees that they were their new bosses. Pearl would be taking charge of the hotel in the morning and Earl would be heading out at first light to get his first look at the Ivanpah Mountains and Kokoweef Peak at long last.

"I am tired," Pearl announced. "Would you mind if I went to the room for a while?"

CHAPTER 27

"GOOD MORNING," EARL said quietly as he noticed the first sign of life the following morning from the mirror where he was shaving. "It is going to be an interesting week. A productive one, I hope."

"What would you like me to do when you are gone?" Pearl inquired as she sat up in bed.

"I am going to talk to James at the livery when I get my horse." Earl informed Pearl. "As long as you are willing, I would like to have you go to Searchlight, possibly with him or someone that works for him. It is 22 miles and should take four to five hours each way so you would have to stay one night."

"What would you want me to do there?" Pearl inquired.

"Look around at the hotels and saloons for ideas. Buy what would make ours look better. Bring back some girls. This town needs girls," Earl instructed.

"You want girls?"

"Of course. I see only one or two in the two small saloons in town," Earl explained. "This town needs a lively place. Not just a place to lean on a bar rail. We have rooms upstairs. Put working girls in them," he further suggested.

"There is a small house next door. Open a brothel. Maybe that would work better later," Earl proposed as he picked up his travel bag.

"Please go as soon as you can. You should be back in two days and likely before my father and brother arrive. I will be back in less than a week," he informed her as he gave Pearl a kiss then turned and exited the room.

He went directly to the mercantile and retrieved the supplies he had requested, including coffee. Pausing to thank Linda, he then continued directly to the livery where James was preparing his horse for the trip.

"I am sending Pearl to Searchlight while I am gone. Would you please see that she has a good wagon and someone to accompany her? She will need to stay one night," Earl instructed James as he approached his horse.

"I could send Linda. My livery assistant can run the mercantile while she is gone. Linda has been there many times for supplies."

"Fine," Earl replied as he mounted his horse.

"You be careful," James cautioned. "Just follow the road along the tracks and you should be at the Cima Station by nightfall. It is 18 miles. Remember Dave. He will help you when you get there."

"Thank you, James," Dorr acknowledged his assistance.

Earl paused to look back at the hotel for a moment then headed down the tracks towards Cima. Meanwhile, in the hotel, Pearl was already readying herself for her trip to Searchlight. Her mind had not stopped since her conversation with Earl. All of her experiences in working for other establishments, good and bad, she could implement into her own. Even having girls working under her. Instead of being the girl.

As mentioned by Earl, there were but two small saloons in the town. These were mostly nothing but meeting places to talk and drink, get drunk, and bed one of the whores. Pearl was to order a piano. One that could be played or as a player piano. She was to order two pool tables. She was to find fine girls. Not like the ones down the street. This was to be the place in town that the miners would come out of the desert for. There would be card tables, roulette, and craps. Those were Pearl's ideas for the place. All of which fell well within her capabilities and past experience. Within an hour after Earl had left town, Pearl and Linda were on their way to Searchlight, Nevada.

Earl found the eighteen miles to Cima easy travel as explained by James. He could see the mountain ranges in the north and to the west in which direction he was traveling. However, from Nipton to Cima was no more than a slight continuous grade as he began to exit the Ivanpah Valley. As the sun began to lower into the west he could begin to see the buildings in the distance that would be Cima. Darkness had fallen with the only light provided by the half-moon that had risen to nearly above his head as Earl rode into the small station site of Cima.

Before nearing the only lit building, Dorr paused to study what he could make out within the shadows provided by the moon. He could make out the outlines of the station building, water tower, and what appeared to be three of the bachelor cabins that Ralph had mentioned. The only other thing he could make out was the startling outline and shadows reflected by the Joshua trees and Jumping Cholla cactus of the area. As the stranger to the area continued to scan the sights unseen by him before, he failed to notice a single shadow that was approaching slowly.

"I would recommend that you freeze in your tracks and identify yourself," a sudden gruff voice warned from the darkness between where Dorr was and the station building.

"I am Earl Dorr. Here from Nipton. I know Ralph at the station there," Earl responded immediately in a loud voice as he squinted in the direction of the voice. All Dorr could make out was the form of a man holding a rifle. That was enough to get his direct attention. The man, to Earl's pleasure, lowered his gun so as to point to the ground.

"Not a good idea to approach any building or campfire out here after dark without announcing yourself immediately," the man warned without moving. "You make sure you are known and make sure that you are welcome before coming closer than yelling distance. Yell until you get a response or stop until daylight," he further warned.

"I am sorry," Dorr responded frozen in place.

"O. K. Come on in. You were very lucky," the man welcomed Dorr to follow and enter the station behind him. Earl tied his horse up to a rail in front of the station and followed the man slowly into the dimly lit station building.

"I suspect a whiskey would be welcome to you following your ride from Nipton and your greeting here?" the man offered.

"Yes. I would be most thankful," Earl responded shyly. "You must be Dave?"

"That be me," he replied with the same gruff voice Earl had been greeted with.

"I would like to water my horse first," Dorr requested.

"At the far end of the rail you tied him to is a water trough. I am sure he has found it by now himself," Dave informed Earl. "Here is your whiskey and bottle for another."

For a few moments Dorr looked about the room in silence as he lifted his shot glass slowly to his lips, moistened them, and followed with his first sip. What he had was a little of everything and not much of anything. A mercantile area with only the essentials; an eating area with two tables; a kitchen in the distance the size for a small house, a bar with but a few bottles and a pool table. There were no signs that a woman had ever set foot in the building.

"I have a deer steak cooking and a bachelor cabin with supplies ready for you," Dave broke the silence as he reentered the room from the kitchen.

"I do really appreciate it," Earl replied showing his gratitude.

"I am sorry for the greeting I gave you," Dave responded abruptly. "I wanted you to know I was serious. If you do not follow the rules out here, you will soon run out of luck and die. This is different than where you are from. It is like it was 50 years ago there. Very dangerous and unforgiving. Follow the rules or die."

"Thank you for the lesson," Dorr acknowledged as he held out his glass in Dave's direction on the way to his own waiting lips.

After eating his wonderful deer steak, Earl and Dave entered into a few friendly games of pool and finished off the rest of the bottle and most of a second.

"Well, it is getting late. I must be off at or near first light," Earl announced.

"Yes. You should," Dave agreed. "Follow me. I will show you to your cabin." Dave moved to the door and lit a lamp that was on a nearby table. He then walked outside, untied Earl's horse, and led the two a short distance to one of the cabins.

"Your horse will be fine in the small corral between the cabins here," Dave informed Earl. "Here, put him in there as I open the cabin up for you," he instructed.

As Dorr led the horse to the corral, Dave opened the cabin door and lit a lantern and placed it on a table near the one bed in the cabin. The bed was large enough for one only, with minimum bedding. Other than a small table next to the bed, there was to be found one more table for eating together with two plain wooden chairs. The kitchen was complete with a small counter, sink, a single area of shelving with supplies and dishes, and a wash basin.

"We will talk in the morning about where you are going," Dave offered as Earl entered the room. "I will answer any questions you have and give directions as best as I can. You look around the cabin. If you plan to be a regular traveler through here, let me know what you would like me to keep available. I will oblige."

Earl thanked Dave as he turned to leave and shook his hand. Earl retired to the bed provided as soon as Dave left. It took awhile of thought before Earl could shut his mind down, but, soon found himself drifting into a deep and needed sleep.

CHAPTER 28

DORR FOUND OUT that it would be very hard to sleep past sunrise in the morning. Only a part of the sun had poked its head above the horizon when Dorr found himself in plain view of all the sun rays shining directly on his pillow. The perfect alarm clock. Secondly, there was a knock on the door just as he realized the sun was on his bed. "Breakfast is ready," a commanding voice could be heard from outside the door. "It will be cooling off in ten minutes."

"O.K. I will be right there," Dorr responded as he threw the covers off to rise from the bed.

"I forgot," the outside voice had returned. "Coffee is on the first step outside your door."

"O.K. Thank you," Dorr responded.

As Earl exited his cabin he went to the corral to feed and water his horse. To his surprise he found that his horse had already been fed and watered and saddled for the trip. He then turned and briskly walked to the station building for breakfast. As Earl entered he was directed by Dave to have a seat and breakfast would be brought out. No sooner said and breakfast was on the table.

"O.K., as you eat," Dave started, "Where are you going and what are you looking for? You can trust me with the info. In fact, you will soon find I will be your guide while you are here. I will answer any questions, guide you, provide all supplies you order and a place to rest and stay any time you need it. You can thank Ralph. It is through him that this service is provided. If you need assistance, I am here. If you need assistance I cannot provide, I will find the person who can provide it to you."

"Hard to believe how helpful you are willing to be," Earl exclaimed.

"Out here you do not have to earn it. You have to earn the right to keep it," Dave explained. "We are a big family out here. We must be there for all who have earned the right to our assistance."

"That is wonderful," Earl exclaimed in appreciation of how they could work together as they do. It was like an association.

"Where are you going? What are you looking for? And when do I expect you back here to check in?" Dave questioned expecting answers.

"I am going to Kokoweef Peak. I am going looking for----" Earl was cut off.

"Looking for the Underground River of Gold, right?" Dave interrupted.

"That is right. How did you know?" Earl questioned suspiciously.

"No one, for a very long time, has been up there," Dave began to explain. "But every couple of years or so, someone comes looking for it without success. I am beginning to wonder if it is one of those things a miner will say to cover up that they are mining. Or that they failed at mining."

"I think it will be different this time," Dorr advised him. "I have a rough map drawn by two Indian brothers who have been to the river. I worked with their grandfather in Colorado. He sent me to San Francisco to get the map. They lost a third brother in the cavern so they can't go back in the mountain."

"Well. I wish you well," Dave congratulated Earl, "You do seem to have a head up."

"From the Station there is a road that runs due north," Dave began his instructions. "Follow that road about one mile," Dave stopped and looked directly at Dorr as he was eating. "You God damned cock sucker," Dave exclaimed angrily. "Don't you think that you should pay attention and write down what I am saying?"

"Ya, sorry," Earl replied. "I guess my coffee is slow to work this morning."

"Go get something to write on," Dave instructed. "It might save your life."

Within ten minutes Earl was back. The table was cleaned of breakfast with the exception of the coffee. Dave was impatiently waiting.

"Did you get the one mile up the road due north past your cabin?" Dave questioned.

"Yes, I have that and am ready to continue," Dorr replied.

"At about one mile," Dave continued, "You will come to a fork in the road and a sign that indicates Emi Water Hole. You take the road that goes to the right. It goes west-northwest and passes Striped Mountain to the south then around Striped Mountain and heads to the north on the east side of the mountain."

"Kokoweef will be about six miles from Striped Mountain," Dave continued. "Once you have passed Striped Mountain you should soon, after about one mile, come upon two wooden stakes marking two graves. From there it will be another mile and you will reach a high point in the road. Look at about two o'clock and you will see Kokoweef Peak. It stands by itself across a lowered plateau in front of you. It will appear to be rising from the far side of this plateau to a point about 1000 ft higher than anything else in the area. You can't miss it."

"The mountain itself is quiet right now. No one is on it rightfully," Dave warned. "Tell them to get off the mountain and come to me for instruction. That is how this area works. You must get a permit from me to go there. You must check in and check out. It is for your safety."

"I will give you a 1500 acre claim for the mountain," Dave informed him. "I am also the Government Land Management Officer for the Ivanpah and New York Mountain ranges. If you tell them to leave and they don't, give them a couple warning shots. They are on your claim. You have a right to shoot them off your claim. Give plenty of warning. Then shoot again. Unless they make it clear that they just want to talk to you, and you agree, shoot to kill if they don't leave. Then come and get me," Dave completed his speech.

"That is why I have warned you," Dave continued. "They have the same right. Ask them to come to you to talk if you need to talk to them. Do not approach them unless they give you very clear permission to pass on to any claim that they may have. They should be well marked. But you could miss it."

"I will be back within three to four days," Earl informed Dave as he mounted his horse and started up the trail towards the north as instructed.

"O.K. See you then," Dave said as he turned and went back to the station.

Earl was now on his first venture towards Kokoweef Peak. Anxiety was building fast inside of Earl for that first sight of what he had come to see. Meanwhile, back in Nipton, Pearl and Linda were about to climb aboard their wagons and head out for Searchlight about 22 miles to the east in the state of Nevada, hoping to return before Earl's father and brother who should be arriving in three days. Their plan was to order what was needed to upgrade the hotel entrance lobby, including lobby desk and four red velveteen chairs and small tables. Also six tables large enough for four people each to eat with comfortable chairs.

For the bar area, six small tables with two uncomfortable chairs. No money made in the bar as they just sit. A crap table, two card tables and chairs would be ordered. They also would order a pool table. They would purchase what was needed to upgrade four of the bedrooms for people of status, and also purchase what was needed to upgrade four other rooms from which the girls they would bring back would work. Other than the wandering girls out on the wooden boardwalk working nearly on their own, this would be a first for Nipton. They had to pay for use of the rooms above the saloons. Pearl and Linda would bring back the working girls and what they could carry. The rest would be delivered in a few days.

Just as Earl was about to part Cima, Pearl and Linda were departing Nipton and heading in the other direction for their shopping excursion in Searchlight, Nevada, 22 miles east of Nipton and across the Colorado River. Searchlight began to boom in 1902 and reached its peak in 1907. At one point the population reached 1,500. In fact, at that time it had a larger population than Las Vegas. In May of 1902, a 16 mile narrow-gauge railroad was built down the hill to the company's mill on the Colorado River. The busiest times for Searchlight were 1907 to 1910. Searchlight was much larger than Nipton at this time. But things did change fast.

There were many gold and silver mines that were excellent producers in the Searchlight mining district. But, most of the gold and silver came from two mines. The Duplex and the Quartette Mines. The mines had supported many stores, hotels, and saloons, but the gold and silver mining cost in 1910, together with the grade of the ore going down, caused the town's population to dwindle.

Being close to the Colorado River, Searchlight began to lean on boat transportation to support the town. Las Vegas was beginning to grow which added to the need for boat transportation together with the rail traffic. Many rail lines such as the Atlantic and Pacific Railroad, a subsidiary of the St. Louis and San Francisco, helped to maintain Searchlight despite the depreciation of the mining that was its original founder. However, the mining districts closer to and around Nipton were at their peak with no sign of failing. Being out of the Colorado River district and farther from more populated areas, mining was still the number one industry of Nipton and the New York and Ivanpah Mountains. This played into the hands of Earl Dorr and Pearl Hart. They needed what was not needed in Searchlight.

Following several hours the girls had crossed the mighty Colorado River and found themselves in Searchlight.

"Who will take us seriously?" Pearl questioned.

"I have an idea," Linda spoke up. "A man by the name of George Frederick Colton pretty much founded Searchlight when he started the Colton and Duplex Mine. I know that they are still running. My husband James worked with him then before moving to Nipton to open the livery and hardware."

That seemed to be not only a good idea, but, the only one that made any sense. It took but an hour to locate the offices of Mr. Colton. "I would like to see Mr. Colton please," Linda introduced herself to a man standing in the office. As the man was explaining how hard it would be to see him a man entered.

"Well. I believe I know this lovely Lady," the man spoke.

"Why. Mr. Colton, how have you been?" Linda inquired as she turned and recognized him.

"What brings you here and what may I do for you?" he offered.

"We need a lot of things. But first, I would like to introduce to you Pearl Hart. She and a Mr. Earl Dorr have purchased the Nipton Hotel and want to upgrade."

"My Pleasure to meet you Ms. Hart," George Colton responded. "Damn. Your name sounds familiar. I travel so much. But, I have no idea where I heard it. Not yet anyway."

"I can show you two very nice hotels that are closed. All inside can be bought. One is set up more on the line of a saloon with a lot of working girl activity and the other quite nice and complete with a stage for shows that could be disassembled easily for travel," Mr. Colton informed them.

"We need much more than we can handle ourselves," Pearl spoke up to question, "Could you introduce us to a company that could transport what we purchase?"

"Of course," he responded immediately. "I use the people at

the Barrwell and Searchlight Railroad. They also transfer by wagon to where rail does not go. Why don't I show you the two hotels. I will open them up for you to look through," he suggested. "I did take ownership when they closed so I am sure we can come to a price that works."

"Mr. Colton?" Pearl asked. "I will also be looking for three or four working girls."

"Speak no more," he replied. "I will find them and send them here to meet with you, O.K.?"

"You are such a blessing," Pearl replied.

"I expect free room, board, and service should I visit Nipton."

"Always. Whatever you please," Pearl promised.

For the rest of the day and into the next, Pearl and Linda inspected all that they could find within the two businesses that would be of use. Tables and beds, bar, mirrored wall shelves for the liquor, pool tables, craps, roulette, tables for card laying, tables and chairs for both the dining room and the bar. Curtains and lights, new lobby desk and even a bench for outside.

A price of $5000 was agreed upon, which was equal to what Earl had given her to spend. Due to the close connection between Linda and Mr. Colton, this part of the transaction went smoothly.

"Hey," Linda and Pearl turned to see who was calling.

"Look what I have," George said. "These four beauties would like to go with you. If you can't make it with them, you are in the wrong business."

With George were four young, beautiful to their fullest, girls dressed in full Victorian. Your first thoughts had to be, "Where in Hell did they come from?"

"I will take all four," Pearl spoke up. "Don't worry," Pearl assured them, "I have done all you will be asked to do and more. I will see that you are very well taken of. You will be working hard at first as we get this started. We all will together. You will be treated with dignity and taken care of. Any man who gives you trouble will never come back. Our place will be a nice place. There are dirty saloons down the street they can go to," Pearl continued her reassurance.

The girls loaded the two wagons that they had brought themselves. One wagon was used mostly for the girls and their belongings. The second wagon was loaded with the lighter items the girls could handle themselves such as bedding, curtains, chairs etc. The rest was being loaded for travel in several wagons that would follow within a day or two.

"Thank you very much and hope to see you in Nipton soon," Pearl invited George Colton.

"I will be there in a few days, I assure you."

At first light all goodbyes were shared and the girls were on their way. It was an easy trip on a traveled road following a rail bed. Two gunmen, driving two additional supply wagons, were provided by Mr. Colton to ensure they made it safely to Nipton. The new girls had offered their services in thanks.

Earl had reached the Emi Well and was to take a road to the right which would take him east northeast then gradually turn to due north to navigate around Striped Mountain with its hazardous climb of nearly seven thousand feet. The road Earl was instructed to take would avoid this completely and would require only a gain of about seven hundred feet. Most of the grade was very gradual as far as he could see from the well. Once he had turned onto the road from Emi Well he could see Striped Mountain ahead and to the west. In the direction he was headed was the Kokoweef Mountain range but Kokoweef Peak had not come into view.

Dorr continued on the road watching the strange vegetation that he had never seen before. Most common were Barrel cactus, Old Man cactus and Joshua trees. On many of the rock outcroppings could be seen clumps of Hedgehog cactus growing in the shadows and within the many dry wash areas. Soon he came upon a pole corral that was likely used to round up range cattle though there had not been any sign of such activity as yet. Looking up the hillsides from the road he could see many signs of old small inactive mines together with a few building ruins.

Dorr came to a sudden stop as he turned a curve in the road around an outcropping and noticed two men on horses blocking the road ahead. After a short pause, he slowly approached in silence stopping but a few feet before them.

"Howdy," one of the men finally broke the silence. "What may your purpose be on this road?" he questioned.

"I am new to the area arriving from Colorado," Earl began "I purchased property in Nipton and am just looking around the area," he further explained.

"May I ask to what business is it of yours?" Dorr inquired with an obvious irritated notion in his voice.

"The business, may it be, is you are a stranger to me," one of the men replied forcefully.

"Look, sir, I ask to pass quietly," Dorr requested. "I have no business with you."

The men remained in Dorr's path requiring him to go round them on the edge of the road.

The men remained silent as Dorr passed with eyes meeting with caution.

"I do not know what your fucking problem may be," Earl paused once safely beyond, "but I suggest it be history should we meet again."

Receiving no response from either man, Dorr pulled on his horse's reins and continued on his way towards Kokoweef Mountain. The episode troubled the concerned stranger to the territory, as Earl Dorr was. However, turning several times to look, he never spotted the men again. Suddenly, as he crested a rise in the road, before him was a wonderful sight. There was Kokoweef Peak. It stood high above the surrounding horizon as if reaching for the clouds above in a 45 degree climb nearly one thousand feet to a perfect point.

Dismounting, Dorr stood in awe. There it was. If only the mountain could talk. What would it reveal? That is the question he had come so far to answer.

CHAPTER 29

IT TOOK SEVERAL more hours for the return trip to Nipton due to the loaded wagons, however, daylight prevailed as the town could be seen before them. As they entered town with their four wagons heavily loaded and four very enticing ladies, in addition to Linda and Pearl, under armed guidance, much attention was given. With the exception of two standing together on the boardwalk in front of taverns that they owned--the "Gold Dust" and "The Shaft"--there were cheers from the men of the town in response to the four waving prostitutes. It was obvious to them that their rundown taverns would not be welcome to the notables of the town.

"Let us place the wagons in the livery once we unload the girls' provisions and worry about the rest in the morning," Linda, owner of the livery, suggested. "They will be safe there."

"That is a good idea," Pearl agreed. "I will ready rooms for the girls and two for the men."

Late into night the drinking and celebrating could be heard coming from the hotel bar and the rooms of the girls as they were busy providing services for the men of the town on their opening night. Unnoticed were the owners of the "Gold Dust" and "The Shaft" taverns as they entered and stood talking softly. They knew the best of the town would no longer be entering their doors. But, the town was growing fast with the many mines that were opening along with the crossroads of traffic and rail, and they would survive. Nipton was, after all, a lawless town.

"Would you have a room available?" a stranger to the town requested of the man behind the counter at the far end of the lobby.

"Let me check for you, sir," he responded. "I am certain that we do."

"Yes, I do have one room," he acknowledged. "Would you be able to double in one room?" the clerk further questioned as he noticed a second man.

"Oh yes. That will be fine. You certainly are busy," he commented. "Is it always like this?" the man questioned.

"No. But, there is celebration tonight by the new owners." he responded in excitement. "May I have your name please?" he requested with pen ready to enter the man's name on the ledger.

"My name be Mark Dorr and this is my son, Joe," he informed.

"We have been expecting you and have a room ready especially for you. May I introduce myself? I am Randy."

"Could you tell me where I might find my son, Earl?" the graying man inquired.

"He has been in the mountains for several days. He should be returning within the next two days," the clerk informed him. "He be looking for something in the Kokoweef Mountains. I can introduce you to Pearl, his girl and manager of his hotel."

"His hotel?" he questioned in surprise. "He owns this hotel? He never mentioned that."

"He bought half interest in it," Randy replied. "I will show you to your room and have your bags brought to you. I will also have a table ready for you. You must be hungry."

He then led the bewildered father and brother of Earl to their room overlooking the main street. The news of the hotel ownership and the absolute wildness of the town in comparison to what they had left in Colorado, left them in disarray to say the least. Soon a knock could be heard on the door as they neared readiness to return to the commotion below.

"Hi, I am Pearl," she introduced herself as the door opened. "May I show you to your table?" she offered.

"Certainly, thank you," Mark replied.

"I understand you and Earl own a share of this hotel," Joe

questioned Pearl as they entered the hallway leading to the stairway.

"Yes, that is correct. We also are quite fond of each other," she further informed him.

With that added information she proceeded to show the men to their table in the dining room.

"Here you are gentlemen. I hope you will enjoy yourselves. You will see a lot of changes in the next few weeks."

Pearl then left the men to their wonderment as they sat in near silence looking at what was around them and what was in store for them. They did notice that a lot of men seemed to be enjoying themselves with the girls. It had been a long day of travel for the men. Once dinner was completed they moved to the bar for a couple of drinks and then retired for the evening. There were certainly a few surprises for them. They had expected to find Earl by himself, waiting for them to arrive with further plans that entailed a range ranch for them and him in search for the Underground River of Gold. As it was, however, they were not certain of anything other than the need for a good night's sleep which could be a task in itself between the noise down in the bar and the squeaky springs in the next room.

"It has been a very long and tiring day," Pearl said with a deep sigh as she walked up to Linda standing near the bar. "I think I will go to the boardwalk for a breath of fresh air then retire for the night."

"Don't go beyond the front of the hotel," Linda cautioned. "It gets rowdy out there this time of night."

"I will be but a few steps from the door," Pearl replied sounding slightly irritated with the thought of the need for a cautionary warning.

The night dance of the desert air created by the rising warmth from the sand heated by the hot day's sun blending with the cooling air as it settles into the valley, can settle the tired mind of any busy day. There just appeared to be a natural romancing feeling as it brushes across your face. So many stars on a moonless night, disrupted only by an occasional streak of light created by the death of a distant star.

"Hi sweetie," a chilling voice shattered the peacefulness. Before Pearl could turn towards the voice an arm slithered around her shoulder as a hand grabbed her left breast. "How about a five dollar piece of that tight ass."

"How about a five dollar piece of this," Pearl responded as she spun around and raised her knee into his balls.

Pearl said nothing as she stood in silence and watched the surprised drunk grab his crotch and sink to the boardwalk on both knees.

"Maybe you should try sucking cock, you pussy," Pearl suggested as she kicked the poor excuse of a man in the head on her way past him and returned to the hotel.

"A whiskey" Pearl demanded as she approached the bar.

"Ma'am, may I speak to you for a moment?" Pearl heard a requesting voice coming from behind her as she raised her glass to take a sip of whiskey.

Slowly she looked up to the mirror in back of the bar and could see it was a man with a star.

"You are lucky I can see that star," she said as their eyes met in the mirror.

"I am Sheriff Beckett. Would you like me to arrest that man or just jail him until he sobers up?"

"Just throw him in the alley. I may want to kick him again," Pearl suggested as she turned to face the sheriff.

"I am Pearl Hart. I am the manager of the Hotel Nipton," she introduced herself.

"I heard we had a new owner," the sheriff acknowledged. "Looks like he picked a very good manager."

"Brought in some new girls, I see. You may have trouble with the other tavern owners," he cautioned.

"From what I see, our girls are of a different class. I think we will cater to a man that would not be happy down the street," Pearl commented. "Possibly they will have to clean their act up a bit."

"Good night, sir. I must retire. Look forward to speaking with you again soon," she said with a smile as she left the bar and headed for the stairs leading to her room above.

CHAPTER 30

THE FOLLOWING MORNING, as Pearl lay in bed with eyes slightly open, she began to become aware of a rather loud engine sound and a commotion which only an excited crowd could create.

"What the Hell is that?" she questioned out loud to no one but herself as she suddenly sat up in her bed.

Slowly she rubbed her eyes and walked to the window overlooking the front street below. What she saw was a sight she and perhaps no one else in the town had ever seen before. A truck. Standing with it was Earl's father and brother and a crowd of men that had gathered around it. Then she began to realize it was the truck that Earl had mentioned that would be coming in on the train with them. The truck was a 1906 Lambert Model A. It had a high clearance with a 115 inch wheel base which would work very well on the roads created by the wagons and stage coaches. The truck also had a bed of nearly 100 inches that could carry a good load of supplies or mine rock. Sitting high behind the engine was a bench seat large enough for three men.

In a few moments her mind returned to the task at hand, unloading the wagons that she had brought from Searchlight and getting the stage reassembled in place in what was to be the showroom. A smile crept across her face as she dressed and realized that she had gained two men who had nothing else to do until Earl returned to town.

Meanwhile, Earl sat as the sun began to rise above the mountain which had been his destination, studying the map the Indian brothers had given him. As he compared it to the actual mountain and terrain surrounding it, he realized he was on the southwest side of the mountain. The entrance would be on the northeast side and a climb of about five hundred feet. Being a small mountain peak rising from the range, it would likely be but a ride of no more than a half mile. He decided to continue on the road to see if it would go past or around the mountain peak. Finding that the road continued on towards the west with no sign of any road or trail for his use in the direction he needed to go, Earl decided to return to Nipton. He knew that there should be a truck there for his use by now or at least soon. That would allow him to transport needed supplies as far as Cima. From there he could then transfer the supplies to the site as needed. Therefore he started the day trip back to Nipton, stopping at Cima to make arrangements for the use of the bachelor cabin.

"Howdy Dave," Earl spoke as soon as he saw Dave approaching. "Thought I would leave a few things here and return to Nipton."

"Any idea when you may return?" Dave inquired.

"I am not sure. Depends on whether or not my father has arrived with a truck." Earl responded. "Either way, it won't be long."

"O.K. See you when you return. Have a good trip," Dave wished him.

Meanwhile, in Nipton, under the direction of Pearl and Linda, the four wagons of supplies from Searchlight were well on the way to being unloaded. The townsmen had joined to assist and were reassembling the stage in hopes of seeing a show that evening. Another group of men were setting up what was to be a very nice dining room for a town such as Nipton. It would include a rather formal area consisting of four tables and an informal area consisting of eight tables. New furniture and admitting counter along with a new bar and settings for six top of the line rooms would also arrive the following day. This day was a day of cleaning and painting.

As evening approached, the hotel was ready for the girls to put on a show for the men of the town. These same girls would also entertain the men after the stage show. The stage show was a good way to arouse a level of interest. All of the needed cleaning and painting was done and ready for the arrival of the rest of the new furnishings in the next day or two. Darkness was about to fall as Earl entered the hotel bar and approached unnoticed the table where Pearl, Mark and Joe were sitting.

"Well, looks like you guys have been busy," Earl announced his arrival as he grabbed a chair and sat at the table between Pearl and his father.

"Been a long time. A long time," Mark said as he put his arm around Earl.

"Yes, Dad. It seems like a long time since I left Colorado."

"Looks like you have a good start for yourself here in this little town," Joe entered the conversation.

"Haven't got anywhere with Kokoweef Mountain," Earl informed them. "I have been to the mountain. I don't think it will take long to locate once I get set up. Have a contact up the tracks about 5 miles where I can store supplies and stay if I want to."

"How about the ranch?" Mark questioned.

"Have been told of one in the New York Mountains north of here about 30 miles. It is very livable and is empty. Owners just abandoned it when their mine ran dry."

"Have you seen the truck?" Joe questioned.

"Yes. I stopped at the train station and Ralph took me to the warehouse to see it. It is a beauty."

"What have you been up to, Pearl? Looks like you spent a lot of money. But, I like what I see."

"There will be more arriving tomorrow," Pearl informed Earl.

"I will take you to the station and have Ralph explain how to get to the ranch. Me? I think I will rent a couple more horses and take supplies to Cima then spend a day or two trying to locate the entrance."

"We just as soon rest a bit for a day or two. Why don't you take the truck," Mark suggested. "Joe and I can stay here and help Pearl get set up. We will also talk to Ralph while you are gone."

"Sounds alright to me. What about you, Pearl?"

"I would but I have more stuff coming tomorrow and must show them were to put it," Pearl reminded him.

"I think I will clean up and get some sleep," Earl informed everyone.

"Don't you want to see the girls dance, Earl?" Pearl suggested.

"When I get back. I will have plenty of time then," Earl replied. "Right now, I would like to clean up and get some sleep."

"I will be up in little while," Pearl answered as she gave Earl a kiss.

CHAPTER 31

AS SOON AS the sun began to show the first rays of sunshine Earl kissed Pearl goodbye and headed towards the mercantile. Finding no one there he headed for the station and found Ralph just in the process of unloading the truck knowing Earl would be up for it soon.

"Good morning, Ralph," Earl announced himself.

"Good morning. I knew you would be along soon, Earl. Thought I would get the truck out and ready it for you."

"I see a light came on at the mercantile. Why don't you go there and check your supplies while I ready the truck," Ralph suggested. "They pulled what they thought you would need. I am certain that you will want to add to it." Earl took his suggestion and returned to the mercantile.

"Ralph said you had most of what I would need gathered already," Earl said as he entered the store.

"I am glad it is you here this morning and not Linda," Earl commented. "I don't want the girls to know some of what I will be taking."

"What might that be?" James questioned.

"If I am lucky, I will need some cave equipment."

"You know better than to go in alone," James warned Earl excitedly.

"I know. I just want to get it out there" Earl assured him.

"What is it that you want, Earl?"

"Two helmets with kerosene head lamp; kerosene; lamp fuse; three hundred foot rope ladder; two hundred feet of rope, two cases dynamite; caps; one thousand feet of fuse; nail hammer; nails;

153 ❧

chip hammer; flares; and three 5-gallon water containers. I will want a canteen and backpack also. Oh. Extra gas cans."

"I can tell you have no idea about going underground," James commented sarcastically.

"Not far. I will go get the truck. Will be right back."

"Truck all set?" Earl asked Ralph as he arrived back at the station.

"Yep. All set. Spare tires, water, oil, and a tool kit," Ralph informed Earl.

Was not long and Earl was on his way to his first stop, Cima, to check in with Dave and leave most of the supplies there, for now.

"Thought I would see you soon," Dave greeted Earl as he pulled into the Cima Station.

"I like your horse. Nice black color," he further made a point of the truck.

"I have the cabin you stayed in last time ready for you Earl. There is an outhouse storage building with that one also," Dave offered Earl.

"By the way, you do have a claim document, don't you?"

"Oh, yes. I also have a copy for you to keep here," Earl told him as he reached into a box and handed Dave the papers.

"That was a good idea," Dave told him.

"Wow. Fifteen hundred acres. Impressive."

"I heard that you had a run-in with a couple of the miners out there," Dave continued. "Keep a low profile until they see that you have your own plan and one that does not include them," Dave warned Earl.

"I will stay away from them unless they invite trouble," Earl assured Dave.

"But, if I see them anywhere on Kokoweef Peak, I will shoot one warning only."

"I will tell them," Dave agreed.

"But there are others," Dave added.

"I will warn them all once," Earl repeated. "My plan is three days. If I am not back by the fourth, come for me, please." Earl requested.

"I will for sure. I will tell anyone I see about you. They will leave you alone if I tell them I know you," Dave assured Earl.

"Here. More flares and also smoke bombs if you run into trouble during the day," Dave added to Earl's load.

"Thank you, very much, Dave. I had better get up there."

"May I suggest something?"

"Of course," Earl replied.

"I have a pack horse. I know it will slow you getting there. But, from what you said, there is no road off the Cima road to where you are going and you have the likelihood of a four to five hundred foot climb," Dave offered suggestively to Earl.

"Hell of a good idea," Earl replied appreciatively.

With that Earl moved the truck closer to the bachelor cabin and transferred what he would not need immediately and, with a wave to Dave, was off for Kokoweef Peak. As he passed Emi Wells and turned right continuing on Cima road, Earl had one thought. That the noise of the truck, which was quite loud in the otherwise quiet of the desert, would quell the suspicion that he was sneaking up on anyone.

Earl was definitely in no hurry as he paused many times to observe the splendor of the narrow road as it wound its way carefully through the rock outcroppings and cacti, some of which required ducking to miss. The gray granite rock prevailed with occasional white veins of quartz flowing through. Quartz veins are always a good sign when looking for gold or silver.

Earl pulled the truck over and stopped. He had seen nice veins of quartz from the road and wanted to get a closer look at them. He started to walk the thirty or so feet to the spot he was looking at. Suddenly, as he reached the spot he heard the crack of a gunshot followed directly by the ping sound of a bullet ricochet off a near rock. Ducking behind a rock and turning immediately, he could see by the smoke where the shot had come from.

"This is bullshit," he thought to himself. Dorr immediately ran back to the truck and reached for his two rifles. Taking aim with both of his Winchester 78 lever actions, he shot both twice. A total of four shots at the location where he had seen the smoke.

"Show yourself now," Earl ordered. "This is your only chance. Then I will wait until I see movement and shoot," he further warned.

"Don't shoot," was his reply. "There are two of us and we will hold our rifles high and come out."

"O.K." Dorr agreed. "But, do it now." Slowly Dorr could see the two men come out from behind a rock ledge with rifles high.

"You keep those rifles high and walk to where I am," Dorr ordered. "I have my eye on you. If I don't like what I see, I will shoot."

Slowly the men climbed down from their spot on the side hill about two hundred feet away. Dorr's rifles were still pointed in their direction.

"Stop right there," Dorr ordered when they had reached a spot within about fifty feet. "What the fuck was that all about?"

"We did not recognize you and have never seen that truck before," one of the men responded.

"Well. I will tell you what," Dorr responded. "I will be traveling this road a lot for a long time. I have claim markers with me," he continued. "You go anywhere on the claim I will shoot one warning shot. The second one, if needed, will kill you" Dorr continued. "You shoot at me again as you did now, the first one will kill you. If you shoot at me again I will not shoot a warning shot. Is that crystal fucking clear?"

"But, we did not recognize you," the man repeated.

"Look, damn it. This is a marked road and you do not own it," Dorr responded. "There are no claim markers between my truck and the spot that I walked to. Get my drift?"

"I will shoot to kill next time," Earl further warned.

Without another word Earl got back into his truck and headed for his destination. Soon he had reached the point in the road where he would have to leave the truck and lead the horse up the five hundred foot climb to where the opening should be. Earl was able to drive the truck around the back side of the peak so that it was not easy to see from Cima Road. From there he loaded the basic needs and began the climb to a point that by triangulation on the map should bring him close to the point of entry. He was aware of the way the Indians cover such a place and also of the special hints of location that no one would have the aid of. He figured 2.5 feet per climbing step would likely take him 200 paces, allowing a few one way or another for climbing over or around rocks. But, there were few large ones in the immediate path he was to follow.

Looking up to his right he watched the rock formations and veins for the varying colors along with the uplifts and fractures. To his right was the high side of the mountain as he climbed across and towards the east-southeast. To his left was a large flat plateau before falling off to a lower level that could not be seen from where he stood. Beyond the naturally formed table to his left was a breathtaking view that had the appearance of going on forever. Beyond the edge of the plateau area, that extended about one mile, could be seen a very large white, flat area which looked like a dry lake bed. Both to the north and the south were mountain ranges.

Once Earl had reached the area he felt should be close, he just sat and studied closely for anything that did not look natural. He was sure, due to the years since, that now nothing would be evident to the eye. Despite the fact that the area was very rocky, the blowing sand over the many years could have accumulated several inches deep along with overgrowth. Though sparse, the small cacti and grasses could hide any evidence very easily.

The first thing to do was move, as much as possible, sand and loose small rocks and look for any sign of a crack or unnaturally lying rocks. This would be slight in evidence and would require carefully looking for anything. The Indians knew very well how to hide and bury. Just a slight crack, however, could show air flow with powdered smoke material lit when poured into it.

Following several hours, Dorr had moved enough sand and small material to make an area appear to be flat with about a four foot straight rise behind it. As he inspected the exposed area he could see that for several feet and with varying heights it continued forming a shelf about five feet wide on which he could walk. Scraping at the bottom of this straight wall produced several cracks and small holes. Using his pick hammer he was able to lift out several small rocks, allowing him to create a very small crevice. Into this crevice he placed three small devices about three feet apart. These devices contained a mixture of an oxidizer, likely potassium chloride, a fuel of sugar, a moderate amount of sodium bicarbonate to slow the burning and a colored powdered dye. The burning mixture evaporates the dye and forces it out of the device.

With luck Earl happened to pick a day with little breeze. Most mornings are that way early. Once the smoke slowed Earl would look for a created flow. It could flow up or it could flow down. He would be very happy with either. If there is a cavity, air will flow. Once the smoke slows, it would be sucked into the cavity. At some point, the air pressure would become equal and the smoke would reverse and flow out of the cavern. The greater the amount of the smoke, together with the velocity of the smoke, can closely indicate the size of the cavern.

After several hours, Dorr had accomplished making one opening large enough for him to reach in, up to his elbow. This was what he wanted. This would allow him to light the device and drop it in for an even flow. With hands shaking in anticipation, Earl lit the device and dropped it into the hole and stood back as red smoke began to flow out with great velocity. He could even notice a roaring sound. After ten to fifteen minutes the smoke slowed to a stop. Then to his amazement, he noticed the smoke reversed and started to flow back into the hole.

There is only one condition that could cause this to happen. When the hole was first opened, the air pressure inside must have been greater pushing the air out. At a point of pressure equalization the flow would reverse until dispensed. What happened next was even more amazing. Earl lit another device and dropped it into the hole. This time a very small amount of smoke came from the hole. After a few minutes, he began to notice a dull roar as the flow of the smoke increased and then was actually completely pulled into the hole.

"Holly shit!" Dorr exclaimed as he backed away and stood up looking at the hole. "That was a shit load of smoke that just got sucked into somewhere," he concluded.

What was he to do now? He thought. This did not prove anything other than the fact that there is a very large hole for all that smoke to fit into. He watched for hours. Absolutely no smoke came back out.

"Well I don't know what. But, I do have something strange down there," he thought out loud to himself.

He did notice that the air that came out at first was very damp and cold. He could not help himself and began to make the hole larger until, finally, he could lie on the ground and reach into the hole up to his shoulder. The hole went straight down and was about five feet wide by three feet. He dropped a small rock into the hole. He could hear it fall as it hit the walls for a few seconds but never heard it hit bottom. Not knowing the depth he decided to return to the truck and get what he needed to descend by rope far enough to see what he may have found.

Returning within a few minutes Dorr immediately found a crack and drove a four foot bevel ended bar into it to allow eighteen inches onto which he could tie a climbing rope. He attached a carbon lamp to his hard hat. After securing the rope around his waist he stepped in position to climb within the black hole below. After testing the rope, he lit the lamp, reached for his pick hammer lying next to him and began his descent.

Once inside, the hole increased in size to eight feet by ten feet. Pausing, he looked down the left wall and could see a floor. Also looking to the right was a floor. Turning to look behind him he saw no floor, meaning the passageway continued straight down. But, knowing he had a shelf to step onto about twenty to twenty five feet below, he continued. Reaching the ledge he found that it was only three feet wide. Lying on the ledge and positioning himself, he turned, and looking over the edge could see he was far from the bottom. Below was a drop of at least one hundred feet to another ledge. He scanned the walls between where he was and the second ledge and saw calcium carbonate flow covering the walls. This told him that a great deal of water had passed into the mountain through the entrance he was in. Also, because this was predominately a limestone area, it told him that there could be a large cavern below.

This was enough for him to see at this time. Because he was out of rope it was time to leave. Once he reached the outside he found enough brush to cover the entrance to the hole and the bar he had stuck into the rock crack and returned to the truck. That was a very positive find. Being very happy, he turned the truck around and headed towards Cima after drawing a sketch of the area so as to identify the claim boundaries and draw a claim map.

As soon as he arrived at the Cima Station, he located Dave and told him what he dared of his find. Dave told Earl to put down the information and that he would submit a 1500 acre claim which would cover the entire mountain. Using the spot Earl indicated he would use it as a central location point for the claim. It would take about a week. The markers that Earl put in the area this day were good for only thirty days as an indication of intent.

Earl drew the map and signed it. Dave also signed and dated

the map. Dave was a BLM registered agent and would hold the claim until the documents were processed.

"Congratulations Earl. Looks like you may have a starting point to go from," Dave commented. "How about a drink?"

"One good one and I am on my way back to Nipton," Earl said as he reached for the bottle.

"It will be dark soon. Why don't you finish the bottle and stay until early morning?" Dave suggested.

"You know something," Earl said as he looked up to Dave, "That sounds like a very good idea."

CHAPTER **32**

THE DAY WAS also busy in Nipton and not quite ready to slow down either. The activity had been non-stop since the sun rose from behind the distant hills as three more wagons arrived in front of the hotel.

"Good morning," Pearl greeted the drivers. "What might you have brought us this morning?"

"We have furnishings for four first rate rooms and for six additional rooms," the first driver responded. "Also a player piano," he added.

"We will take the piano here in the hotel lobby," Pearl instructed. "The room furnishings will go up in the rooms. But, I have made an arrangement with the owner of the small building next to us to put what is now in the rooms over there. We will be leasing it for a brothel."

"I know where I am going to stay the next time I come to town," the driver responded.

"That's the idea," Pearl responded with a smile as she whisked herself away to the hotel.

The hotel had really taken on a fresh look. With the help of Mark, Joe, Linda and James, Pearl had the showroom ready; a dining room divided into two classes completely ready for dinner; ten sleeping rooms and living quarters done including the lavender drapes in the windows. Unknown to Pearl or Earl, Buck and Oliver Peysert would arrive on the next train from San Francisco. The plan was for them to help Mark and Joe run the ranch when they get one. They may be of help to Earl also but it would not be at the mountain as they cannot go on the mountain that still holds their brother's body.

"The train is arriving," James announced as he entered the hotel lobby.

"Come on, Joe," Mark directed. "Let's go and meet them."

Indians still were not completely welcome by some of the town's population. But, after several years in the San Francisco area, it was hoped they could blend in without too much problem. They would only be there until a ranch was located. Mark and Joe arrived at the station just as their friends were disembarking.

"Over here," Joe yelled waving his hands.

"We have a room at the hotel ready for you," Mark informed them. "After you freshen up you may join us for dinner. Earl is at the mountain but should be back tonight or tomorrow."

"Has Earl had any luck yet?" Oliver inquired.

"He had plans to start looking for the entrance to the caverns on the trip to the mountain he is on now," Joe answered. "We haven't heard yet."

"Pearl, this is Oliver and Buck I told you about," Mark introduced them.

"Welcome to our hotel," Pearl responded. "Earl will be very glad to see you. Follow me, I will show you to your room." Pearl led them up the stairs and made sure they were comfortable.

"Will you join us for dinner?" Pearl offered.

"No. But thank you," Oliver answered after a pause. "We ate on the train and are tired. You eat. We may come down later to join you."

"O.K., as you please."

"Must be about show time," Pearl said as she sat at the table for dinner with Mark and Joe.

The showroom was set up so that there was a row of tables large enough for eating in front of the stage and several rows of chairs behind for watching. Dinner was served. The ladies on stage danced and sang, getting yells and cheers with each kick of their legs. This was certainly the type of evening the town needed. Not much fun resulted from time spent at the "Gold Dust" or "The Shaft" with fights and cheaters for card dealers the norm.

The show lasted for what seemed to be hours with the girls taking turns with their dance and singing routines. As the show continued there was a slow procession of new faces showing up to replace any that left. It was obvious what was going on as the show ended and some of the men made their way to the rooms upstairs. Those who stayed were treated to a continuous flow of drinks in celebration. The drinks flowed. The piano still played. The drunk men were singing now, but in jubilation. As it became evident that Earl was not arriving until morning, all decided that it would be good to retire early and be ready for another busy day.

CHAPTER 33

AS MORNING ARRIVED, those awake could hear the sound of Earl's truck approaching. Shortly after Earl left the truck at the station storage building, he entered the dining room and joined, to his surprise, everyone he wanted to talk to including the Indian brothers.

"The time has come for us to have a serious meeting," Earl began. "I have found what I believe is the entrance to what I am looking for. I must therefore turn my attention to that for a while. You have all met Pearl. She is in charge of the hotel. We also have secured the old house next door for which she also has a use. The hotel is making money. She has other plans for that. I must talk to her but the hotel is now established. I have not been to the location that Ralph has told me about. But, from what he says that will take care of the cattle ranch."

"Dad, I need W. P. Morton here right away. Can you arrange that?"

"Yes. He is aware and waiting for a call," Mark answered. "He will be on the way immediately. I will go and notify him as soon as we are done here." W. P. Morton was a friend of the family and a very experienced mining engineer. Earl's announcement told all that he was moving on exploring the cavern.

"We have done a good job keeping this quiet with the help of the hotel and ranch. They have no idea why I am really here." Earl added.

"Dad. The road to the ranch is a well-traveled road. There is an auto carriage in the station storage that you could use at the ranch if you like. I need the truck for the other project for a while yet. Another week at least," Earl notified him. "Why don't you get the truck loaded with what you want to take to the ranch and we can make a trip there to see if you want to stay there," Earl suggested. "You will have full use of it free."

"Pearl, we need to talk," Earl said turning his attention to her. "Let's go up to the room."

Taking her hand the two walked quietly up to their room and closed the door. As Mark, Joe, and the Indians loaded what they needed into the truck, Earl and Pearl were up in their room talking.

"Is there something wrong?" she asked.

"No. Absolutely not. You have done wonderfully," he assured her.

"Do you feel you will be O.K. if I am gone for an extended amount of time?" he asked. "I will be coming to town occasionally but will not be able to set a schedule. Not now."

"I will be fine," she assured Earl.

"I worry. I know about the drunk who messed you up. I know where to find him and will take care of him before I leave."

"Also," Earl continued, "I know the plan you have with the girls you brought from Searchlight. I am O.K. with it with one exception. They can warm up their clients with their shows and dancing. They can sit on their laps and drink with them. But, when it comes to fucking I want it out of here and in the house next door. That is what it is for. That will separate the two activities and add to the business."

"I promise that that is the way I will manage it," Pearl assured Earl.

"I must do some things now" Earl said, "But I will return before I go away again and have my way with a piece of that," he said as he grabbed her ass.

"I will be waiting," she assured him. "You might even get a blow job. In fact, let me take care of that now," as she opened his pants, pulled his penis out and slowly placed it in her mouth.

"I must take them up to the ranch," Earl told Pearl as he re-dressed himself. "I will be back by dark. It is about 60 miles round trip."

"O.K.," Pearl responded. "Be careful."

With a kiss goodbye Earl left the room and returned to the first floor.

Seeing his father in the dining room, Earl stopped short of the front door. "I will switch and use the touring car as soon I get the supplies I need out to the site. I will have the claim marked by the end of the week. Then I can get started."

"That will be fine, Earl."

"Now for the next business at hand. The drunk that manhandled Pearl. I must deal with that."

He knew his name, Leroy Brown and that he was usually at the "Gold Dust" or "The Shaft." Earl had never been in either or had the privilege of meeting the owners. Larry of the "Gold Dust" or Tim, the owner of "The Shaft."

Earl entered the first of the two, "The Shaft," knowing he would not be exactly welcome there. Looking around, he could see the difference from their hotel immediately. The place was dirty and run down, likely somewhat as the hotel was before Pearl fixed it up. The tables and chairs seemed of unfinished wood. The bar covered with spilled drinks and a spittoon full if not running over. There were half naked girls walking around or leaning on something. Some having various forms of sexual activities within sight of all.

"Christ," Earl thought to himself. "This place stinks like hell."

"Where is Leroy Brown?" he asked the first man he came to.

"He is at the hold-em card table. But I wouldn't bother him," was his answer.

Earl paid no attention. As he walked up behind the man indicated to be Leroy, Earl announced himself.

"Nice hand. Do you know how to play it?"

Earl could see the man's arm move into a position indicating he had a gun and also noticed the others at the table backing away. Without a word, Earl grabbed him in a headlock, took his gun from his holster and hit the man on the side of the head with the gun drawing blood. Throwing the gun to the floor, Earl commenced to drag the man, still in a headlock tight enough that he could not talk, and pulled him out of the chair and dragged him across the floor and out the front door. Throwing him to the dirt street, Earl looked down at him.

"Think you can put a hand on my girls or is it only pussy you can beat up?"

"Fuck you," the man said as he stood in front of Earl.

"I wouldn't say that again if I were you," Earl warned.

"I said, fuck y---."

Without a word or sign of warning Earl sent one left hit to the mid-section quickly followed with a right to the chin and he couldn't finish the word.

"I don't want trouble," Larry, the owner spoke up. "But, we must talk or there will be a lot of trouble."

"Ya. But not now. I will kill anyone who touches any one of my girls," Earl warned. "That is a promise."

As Earl started to return to the hotel he could hear footsteps following.

"What is it?" Earl asked as he stopped and stood without turning.

"I asked that we may talk," Larry requested once again.

Earl turned and looked Larry sternly in the eye. "It is obvious that you run a place much different than I intend mine to be. There is no reason for us to get in each other's way."

"O.K.," Larry responded. "We will see."

Both men turned and began to walk back to their place of business. But Earl hesitated and turned towards the retreating owner.

"I will be out of town. Stay the Hell away from my place and my woman," he warned.

Earl stood in silence and watched as the man continued walking and entered his saloon without responding. That was quite unsettling to Earl but what could he do?

"I will keep an eye on her for you. Don't worry," a calming voice broke the evening silence from the darkness across the street from where the men had been having their contentious conversation. Earl stopped and turned towards the direction of the voice and noticed the sheriff walking towards him.

"I would certainly appreciate that, Sheriff Beckett."

"Just call me Jeff. Please."

"Would you join me for a drink?" Earl offered.

"It would be my pleasure."

"John. Bring a bottle of the best bourbon to our table, please."

"Yes sir," he responded reaching for a bottle from the top shelf behind the bar.

"Have a seat, Jeff," Earl offered.

"I will return directly. I will go to the room and see if Pearl can join us. I don't believe you two have met. Have you?"

"Not directly," the sheriff replied.

"Excuse me," Earl excused himself as he went to their room above.

"Here is your bottle," John announced. "Let me pour you a drink."

John continued to pour the sheriff a drink, as well as Earl, in a glass placed in front of the chair across the table from where the sheriff was sitting. As he waited for Earl to return, he looked around the room slowly sipping from the glass then returning it to the table. Placing his hat on the table, he refilled his glass and continued admiring the changes that had been made to the interior of the hotel since the last time he had been in it.

"Sheriff Jeff. I would like to introduce you to Pearl," Earl announced startling the sheriff who had drifted into thought as he looked about the room.

"My pleasure," he responded as he rose from his chair. "Please sit."

"Thank you," Pearl said as she sat in the chair the sheriff had pulled back from the table.

"You have done a wonderful job fixing up this old hotel," he complimented her.

"Thank you," Pearl responded. "We want it to be a nice place for anyone to come to. Our girls will be respectful. Other than the dancing and singing that they will be performing, their other business will be behind closed doors. Not out to be seen as in the other places."

"I am certain we will have no problems of that nature here," Jeff replied. "It will be a nice change to have a place such as yours to come to."

"What I want is for you to feel comfortable coming to me if you are in need of anything or if a problem arises," he reassured Pearl.

"We both thank you for that," Earl said as he refilled their glasses.

"Do you know who I am?" Pearl inquired.

"I have heard of you," the sheriff replied. "Don't worry. That is not a problem. In fact, it makes me feel confident that you will able to care for yourself just fine."

"You paid your time for what you did," the sheriff assured Pearl.

"But, I am here if you need me," he reminded her. "By the way," he continued. "Will you be performing the skit as you have in other cities reenacting what you became famous for?"

"It does seem to follow me," Pearl replied.

"Well, I think it be time for me to walk the street," the sheriff said as he stood from his seat.

"We must move on also," Earl replied. "Thank you for joining us."

"It was my pleasure," the sheriff replied as he put his hat on and headed for the front door. "It is important that we know each other. I feel you are the people we need here. I will watch over her in your absence," he repeated to Earl as he turned and left the hotel with a tip of his hat.

"Are you ready?" Earl asked as he reached the truck where Mark, Joe, and the Indian brothers were standing. "O.K., let's get going," Earl suggested. "I will lead with the auto wagon. You can drive the truck."

"O K., Let's go'" Earl commanded with a wave of his hand and headed down the Nipton-Ivanpah Road. Following closely behind was the truck.

The Nipton to Ivanpah Road was actually the road to Cima. Ivanpah just happened to be half-way between. Ivanpah was another train station but had closed when most of the mines in the New York Mountains had closed. Most stations, with the exception of Cima, opened and closed with the mine activity. Cima was needed for water due to the Kokoweef and Meskels Ranges.

Once they reached the Ivanpah station they had to turn onto a more directly southern road for five miles to Slaughterhouse Wells where the ranch was at the base of the New York Mountains and near the river fan of Keystone Canyon. As they neared Slaughterhouse Wells they found a ranch house, barn and horse corral complete with horse loading ramp. All in much better shape than expected. They tested the wells and found that there was enough water in all three as they received their water from the New York Mountains directly to the east and south.

"This will work real well," Earl's father exclaimed excitedly.

Looking west and back to the north was open flat land with ample growth for a herd of cattle. Searchlight was a day's ride for supplies and had a cattle auction there once per month.

"Well, I must get back to Nipton," Earl announced as soon as the vehicles were empty. "Must reload and get up to Kokoweef as soon as Morton arrives."

Now with the ranch settled, Earl could get back to Kokoweef. He had to reload the truck and head for Cima and then Kokoweef and see what had to be done while he waited for Morton to arrive which would be but two or three days at most.

CHAPTER 34

THE FOLLOWING MORNING was the beginning of what would be the next chapter of the Legend of the Underground River of Gold. Earl's father and brother together with the Indian brothers were now at their cattle ranch thirty-five miles south near the New York Mountains. Pearl had her hotel to maintain and run as well as the brothel in the house next door to the hotel. It would only be a few days before W. P. Morton would arrive. Instructions were left by Earl for him to stay at the hotel and that a message be sent to Cima announcing his arrival. Earl would be there or at the claim site and returning to Cima every second day.

"Well, James, I think I have all that I can get into my truck for this trip," Earl acknowledged as James approached the truck where Earl was finishing up securing his load.

"If you find you need anything just have Dave send a gram and we will have it ready for you when you return to town," James said. "You can feel confident that Linda and I will keep an eye on Pearl," James promised. "If you hear nothing, there is nothing to worry about. You just be careful and take care of yourself."

"I will. And you know how much I appreciate you and Linda," Earl replied as they exchanged a handshake, hug and pat on the back.

"Earl," Pearl announced as she walked as fast as she could from the hotel towards Earl.

Earl stepped down from the truck seat he had climbed to and stood beside the truck as Pearl approached.

"I know we said our goodbyes," Pearl said. "But, I have one thing more that I want to say."

Reaching out to Earl and placing her arms around his neck, she looked up into his eyes as she softly said for the first time to anyone for many years, "I love you," as tears appeared about her cheeks.

"I love you too," Earl replied shyly.

Following a hug of several moments, Earl reached out for the truck with one hand, kissed Pearl, and climbed into the seat.

"Goodbye, dear," Earl said softly as he shifted gears and started down the road turning to wave.

Soon the dust was all that could be seen as the truck began the short journey to Cima.

"Hi Dave," Dorr announced as he entered the Cima station. "Everything get done at the land office as far as the claim goes?"

"Yes," Dave assured him. "Here are the documents and the maps that you will need to place the triangular post marking the claim."

"Good. I am ready," Earl thanked him as he reached for the papers. "I will be unloading the truck into the cabin and heading to the site. My partner, Mr. Morton, will be arriving in Nipton soon. When he does I will go and get him and bring him here."

For the following few days as he waited for Morton's arrival, Earl fully readied the cabin at Cima and the site at Kokoweef. The site at Kokoweef would be only a camp site so as not to attract attention. The rest of the equipment and supplies needed could wait until Morton arrived. Until that time he spent the days improving access to the site from the Cima road.

The time passed slowly as Dorr was becoming very anxious to enter the caverns. In Nipton Pearl was ready to perform her first reenactment of the stagecoach robbery. Up until now the girls from Searchlight had been the only shows and something new was needed. The showroom filled as word spread throughout Ivanpah Valley and miners in the surrounding hills heard of the infamous lady stage robber, Pearl, and of the upcoming performance. The brothel had become very busy as well. This, of course, was not making the other saloon owners happy as they had lost many of their regulars. Pearl watched over the girls' well-being as best she could.

"Come on in," Pearl responded as she heard a knock on the door to her room.

"What the fuck happened to you?" she asked with shock as Judy, one of her working girls, entered the room. She was bleeding from her nose and had a swollen cheek that looked as if it would soon result in a black eye.

"Sit," Pearl instructed as she pointed towards her bed. She then got a towel and soaked it in her water basin.

"One of the son-of-a-bitches beat up on me for no reason. I think he just likes to hit women," she explained to Pearl.

"Do you know him?"

"Yes. He is Emit Johnson. He usually spends his time at the other saloons but came here for the show then asked for a $5 piece of ass," she explained. "He just laughed and said he was going back to where he could get a better blow."

Pearl continued nursing her injuries with the cold water. A facial expression of intense anger began to become very obvious. This was the first time one of her girls had gotten hurt.

"You stay here," Pearl instructed as she handed Judy the towel. "I am going to take care of him."

Without another word Pearl grabbed her pistol and headed directly out of the hotel. Sheriff Beckett noticed her as she walked through the hotel lobby and followed her as she walked towards the saloons.

"What are you up to, Pearl?" he asked. Pearl did not reply.

"Is Johnson here?" Pearl inquired loudly as she entered the "Gold Dust" saloon.

"He is at 'The Shaft'," one of the working girls answered. Pearl turned and left without speaking a word.

"What are you doing?" the sheriff again asked as he grabbed her arm.

"He beat up one of my girls and I am going to show him what happens when someone does that," she responded as she yelled her response.

"Let me take care of it," he demanded.

"No. I can take care of my own problems and it's best that they know it," she insisted as she pulled her arm away and continued towards "The Shaft."

She had never been in "The Shaft," only the "Gold Dust" which was nothing but a saloon with a card table. "The Shaft" was larger and had rooms on the second floor for its working girls.

"You wait out here by the door," she requested. "Let me show them that I can take care of myself."

"I will be in if I feel something is not right," the sheriff told her.

As Pearl walked inside she could feel the eyes looking at her. To her surprise she could also feel fear trying to overcome her.

"I want no trouble. But I want to see Johnson. Where is he? I know he is here," she questioned the bartender.

"Ya. I heard he was at your place," the bartender answered. "He said he had a real good time."

"Where the fuck is he?"

"He is up in room 4 but I think he is busy right now," he told her.

Without a word Pearl turned and started up the stairs towards the door that was marked 4. Without knocking she opened the door and walked in.

"Well. This is a pleasant surprise. Didn't know that you put out too," Johnson responded as he recovered from his surprise. As he started to walk towards Pearl she pointed her gun at him.

"Hey. That is not a good idea," he said. "I didn't hurt her that much."

"No one is going to hurt my girls," Pearl responded. Without hesitation she lowered her gun to crotch level and fired one shot.

"If there is anything left to it, it will be a long time before you use it again," Pearl said as she turned and left the room.

Behind her was Johnson, lying in a fetal position on the floor holding what was left screaming words beyond recognition. As she walked down the stairs and through the saloon not a sound could be heard. As she reached the door where the sheriff was standing she stopped and turned to look at those sitting in silence. "That is what happens if anyone hurts one of my girls," Pearl warned. No one responded. They just sat in silence.

By now the screaming had turned to crying. Pearl looked towards the room he was in and could see he had crawled to the door.

"Someone had better help him," she suggested as she turned and left the saloon accompanied by the sheriff.

"You are a tough girl," he said. "But, it could get you in trouble."

"They cannot be allowed to think that they can push me around just because I am a girl. They cannot be allowed to think they can hurt my girls. They cannot be allowed to think that I can't take care of myself," she made known.

"I think that you delivered the message," the sheriff agreed.

"I think it would be best if this were not reported to Earl," Pearl suggested. "He need not have this to worry about right now."

CHAPTER 35

THE FOLLOWING DAY W. P. Morton arrived in Nipton. He was given word that Earl would come to get him but decided to hire James from the livery to take him to Cima to save time. A telegraph was sent to Cima requesting a return message as to what further supplies were needed. Morton had brought with him the needed equipment such as altimeters and pedometers as well as instruments to take measurements of distance by triangulation. Together with such instruments, they could make examinations, observations, and estimations.

Once they had the wagon loaded, James and Morton left promptly for Cima. On arrival at Cima, they stopped at the station and had a short meeting with Dave. Dave filled them in as to what had been transpiring, showed them the cabin that Earl was using, helped them to unload what was to stay and add what was needed at the site. He then brought them back into the station for food and a final instructional meeting.

"Earl has been up there for quite some time over the past several months," Dave began. "He has everything ready for the exploration. He has the entire site that was once an area of no excavation or road and has put in an easily navigated road and area at the site leveled by hand."

"The claim site is fully marked including no trespassing signs," he continued. "Signs do not always do much good out here but he has had little problem up until this point."

"Well. You had better be getting up there," Dave concluded. "I know he expects you there today and he wants to be well into the cavern today."

"Are you sure you are up to this Mr. Morton?" Dave asked as he directed his attention to the man well into his 50's.

"I may slow Earl down a little, but I think I will be O.K.," he assured him. "It matters not. I would die happy doing what I will be doing concerning this."

"All right then," Dave said as he headed for the door to walk with them to the wagon. "I have two men that I will send up there looking for you if you do not report back by the end of the sixth day. That was an agreement between Earl and me."

"Sounds good," James responded. "Let's get on our way. Right fork at the wells and follow the Cima road until we see the road to Kokoweef Peak."

"That is right," Dave said as he waved them off. "There is a sign marking the road. Take the sign down as you pass it. We know how to get there without it if we have to."

"O.K., see ya soon," Morton said as the wagon pulled by four horses headed out.

It was about 2 PM when they reached the point in the road where they found the sign marking the way to site. Pulling the sign they continued on the road as instructed. The road circled the west side rounding onto the north side of the peak. Once forty yards within the north side, the road made an abrupt right turn and started a steep climb of about twenty five degrees straight up the mountain side. After a climb of about two tenths of a mile they came to a flat landing about twenty feet by fifty feet. Here they found another sign that read: "Park the wagon. Fire three rounds to signal you are here and wait for me. Earl." They fired the three shots and waited. Within about fifteen minutes they could see a man appear about five hundred feet up the side of the mountain. He motioned and began a descent down to where they were waiting.

"Welcome," Earl greeted his guests. "How was your trip, Morton?"

"The trip was fine and I am ready to get this started."

"How are things in Nipton and how is Pearl doing?" Earl questioned James.

"All is going just fine. Nothing for you to worry about," James answered deliberately not mentioning Pearl's run in with the man the night before.

"O.K. There is a cabin over there," Earl pointed out. "Let's put everything we will not take in the cavern with us in there. The cabin belonged to Pete Ressler. He no longer uses it and no one will know we are. The rest we can stack here until we are ready."

For the next two hours the men separated the supplies and equipment and checked to be sure they had everything they needed. They had kerosene lanterns, both carried and attached to their hard hats. They also carried several stakes with creosote soaked brush roots that would be placed along their path of descent at planned distances in the event they needed them for light if they run out of kerosene. They had their altimeters, pedometers, and other equipment for distances and the like. Plenty of paper and markers. Extra clothes. The temperatures would not be a problem as it would be constant at 58 to 62 degrees with high humidity. Plenty of food and water and, of course, whiskey.

"We are ready," Earl announced as they placed all their gear into backpacks. "Remind Dave that by the end of the fourth day he must hear from us or come and find us."

"I will. He had mentioned it before we left there," James told him. "I will check by telegraph with Dave every day in case you need something. Good luck and be careful." James started his return trip back to Cima and then Nipton as Earl and Morton began their climb to the cavern entrance. Once they reached the entrance they tied both backpacks to a rope that was securely tied to an iron pole pounded well into the ground and slowly lowered themselves into the cavern.

"This will lower us to about fifty feet," Earl informed Morton. "At that level we will have to adjust it for the drop to another level. This rope is two hundred fifty feet. We can leave it there and then begin using another that I have at that level," Dorr informed Morton.

Finally ready, the men disappeared within Kokoweef Peak and began their long awaited exploration.

CHAPTER 36

DORR AND MORTON FOUND a small ledge at a depth of about eighty feet. They secured the rope by wrapping it around an outcropping and continued into the darkness below. Within another forty feet they reached a second and slightly larger ledge. At this point a small hole could be seen in one wall.

"Why don't you wait here and I will crawl into the opening to see if it goes anywhere," Dorr suggested.

"All right," Morton agreed. "I will give you thirty minutes. Then I will come in to find you."

Dorr climbed up about ten feet and leaned into the opening. He could see a space of five feet to a second opening across a drop of at least twenty feet before it narrowed and disappeared into blackness at the bottom. Reaching for the second opening Dorr pulled himself in and found a large room that appeared to be about sixty feet top to bottom and twenty five feet wide. What was impressive was what looked to be white popcorn covering nearly the entire surface of all of two walls. Upon closer inspection he could tell it was a formation of crystallized calcium carbonate or limestone. This would indicate water condensation, but not flow, had formed this beautiful white natural genesis.

Determining that this was a dead end Dorr returned to the original passage where Morton waited and continued another fifty feet to a third ledge. Seeing no openings they continued to a fourth ledge about sixty feet further within the mountain. Looking up from this ledge they noticed a formation of limestone on the wall across from where they stood that appeared as if it were a frozen waterfall of about thirty feet top to bottom.

"That is an impressive sight," Earl commented.

"It certainly is," Morton agreed. "A lot of water flowed through this passageway to form that."

"That is for sure," Earl added. "That water went somewhere."

"Well, let's keep going and see if we can find where it went," Morton suggested.

The two explorers continued until they were at a depth of about one thousand feet where they found another division. Following a short side exploration, however, they found one narrowed to a closure after about only one hundred twenty feet and returned to the original and continued further, deeper into the mountain. Soon they noticed more movement in the air and dampness from below.

"I think we are getting close to something," Dorr commented. "What does the altimeter indicate now?"

"We are close to two thousand feet below the surface," Morton replied.

"You know something," Earl said. "If you really listen, it sounds like water."

"Yes it does," Morton agreed. "Almost like a waterfall."

"Come on. Let's keep going," Dorr said with a noticeable tone of excitement in his voice.

They did not have to go far for the answer.

"Hold on there," Morton warned.

Lowering to his knees, he slowly inched his way in the darkness lit only by his helmet lamp. Soon he could see nothing but darkness.

"There is nothing ahead of me," Morton exclaimed. "My lamp is reflecting off nothing. Give me a rock. I want to throw it ahead of me to see what we have."

As soon as Earl handed him a rock he raised his arm and threw it ahead of him. He listened. After several seconds he heard a very faint thud.

"Damn. That is a long way down there," Morton said in

amazement. "Give me another rock," he requested, "and I will time it."

Dorr handed him another rock and he let it fall. This time he threw it as far as he could to try and clear everything and started to count as he saw the rock pass his light beam that was level with them.

"I get 14 seconds," Morton said after he heard the rock hit bottom.

"How far is that?" Dorr inquired.

"Well, let's see. D=.5(x)32(x)t squared. That is about 3136 feet," Morton responded.

"We found it," Earl responded in jubilation.

"How the Hell can we get down there?" Earl questioned.

"We will have to find where the Indians went down. They must have chipped footings into the rock wall wherever they couldn't climb down," Morton responded.

As they searched the surrounding area they found that the passage they used intersected the cavern about twenty feet from the ceiling and that there was a ledge about four feet wide running some distance in both directions from where they were standing. Knowing that the Indians must have used creosote oil from the creosote bush that was plentiful in the area, there must be black residue on the walls where they once traveled. This proved to be not as easy as they first thought. Over the years the dampness and actual condensation pretty much washed the black residue from the walls. Looking very closely, however, with time they trained themselves to recognize the stains that remained within the crevices of the walls however faint they may have become. Following the stains they found a path about thirty feet from the opening that included steps carved into the rock that led at least to a lower level at about 20 to 25 degrees pitch. If it stayed that way it would be a long but negotiable climb.

"You know something," Earl spoke up. "You add all this up and we will be almost a mile underground."

"You are right," Morton agreed.

"I think we should go back into the passageway and get some rest before we tackle that climb," Earl suggested.

So ended the first day of their amazing adventure into the cavern. They could not see the bottom but could hear water. So they at least knew it likely was a river.

CHAPTER 37

FOLLOWING SEVERAL HOURS sleep and some food, the two explorers were ready to tackle the climb to the floor of the cavern and hopefully the River of Gold. They let themselves down one shelf at a time as the switchback path that the Indians had created was now leading them. As they progressed towards the bottom they began to find plenty of placer sands on each shelf. The sands were reaching a depth of two feet in some areas.

After eighteen hundred feet of limestone shelves they reached granite and found a fault that led through the granite to the bottom of the cavern. Here they found a flowing river that was nearly three hundred feet wide and quite deep. One curious aspect they discovered was that the river water level rose and fell, suggesting that it was a part of a vast subterranean system connected eventually with the Pacific Ocean in tune with its tidal movement. Exposed on both sides of the river was one hundred to one hundred fifty feet of black sand beach that looked to be very rich in gold. The sands varied from four to fourteen feet in depth.

Over the following two days the two explored the cavern for eight miles. For the entire length there was little variation in depth or width of the sands. This means that there was no less than three hundred to three hundred fifty feet of rich placer sands likely bearing gold with an average depth of eight feet. Returning to the surface far above proved to be a far more debilitating task than they had envisioned due to lack of foresight likely resulting from the anxiety they felt leading up to their experience.

Fortunately the men had placed provisions and needed supplies for the return trip at strategic locations. They had planned

very carefully as they progressed lower into the network of pas-
sageways and caverns on a daily basis and on their experiences
that they had encountered. This planning allowed for them to have
to carry only the minimum and leaving behind as they go what
they needed no longer or that they could replace. The only additional item that would make its way to the surface was a ten pound
sample of the black sand needed for an assay report. They had
loaded themselves up with much more gold laden black sand but
that was soon to be left behind as they made their climb. The steep
and arduous climb up the cavern walls and over cliffs and what
seemed to be endless crevices, soon became too much for Dorr's
partner. It was all that Dorr could do to help him to the surface.

No estimate was made at this time of the approximate tonnage
of the black sand, but as the assay report would include an estimate based on cubic contents for the more than eight miles and
average depth of what appeared to be never less than three feet, it
was deemed unnecessary. The assay report was to be determined
based on two and one-half pounds of the black sand and proved
to have a value of $2,145.47 per yard, at a gold value of $20.67
per ounce.

Because it had been four days since Morton had left Cima to
meet Dorr, Dave had become very worried. Earl was way overdue
to return. Not being able to leave the station, Dave requested that
two men, known as Slim and Shorty, go and find them. He gave
them the directions but not the actual location of the cavern entrance. The mistake that Dave made was not to think about the fact
that Earl did not know these men. It likely would not go over very
well with Earl that two strangers knew the entrance location.

The searchers, Slim and Shorty, found the mountain location
and found where the truck and wagon had been left. They also
found evidence of Dorr and Morton having been there. As the
two were looking about the area of the truck and wagon, Dorr
had reached the entrance opening and had climbed out and sat

next to it attempting to catch his breath before helping Morton out. Suddenly, he noticed the two men, strangers to him, walking towards the path that led to the entrance.

"Reach up to me," Earl instructed to Morton. "I need to get you out of there."

He reached into the entrance and grabbed Morton's hand. Morton had become exhausted and was in very bad shape and unable to cope with the rigors of what they were required to do during the past four days and capped by the extreme climb to get out of the cavern. Dorr was unable to get him out and found himself in need of the help of the two strangers.

"Please come up here," Dorr yelled to the two men. "My engineer is in bad shape and I cannot get him out myself," Dorr responded.

"Do you have rope?" one of the men said.

"Yes," Dorr responded. "I just do not have the strength to pull him out by myself."

Once they reached the entrance they took over for Earl and after they tied Morton to the rope they pulled him to the surface.

"We must get him to the truck so I can take him to Cima and maybe to Nipton for medical attention," Earl instructed.

Slim grabbed Morton under his armpits while Shorty grabbed his legs and then lifted the now unconscious engineer and carried him down the side of the mountain to the truck. They were in the process of lifting and shoving Morton into the truck when some of the black sand that the engineer had selected to save from the river, and had put in his pockets, spilled out. Being familiar with black sands and gold they recognized the gold immediately. The men told Dorr that he must have something wrong with the claim border because the entrance was actually on land that a miner named Pete Ressler owned. He would not be happy with Dorr and Morton going into the cave or taking anything out of it. So Dorr had a real problem. It was now known about the gold and it appeared that the entrance to the cavern could be on someone else's property.

Dorr had no choice but to take Morton and get help for him. Leaving Slim and Shorty, Dorr drove to Cima where he told Dave the problem he had about Morton.

"I can't help him," Dave replied to Dorr. "You had better take him to Nipton."

The doctor at Nipton did what he could but advised that Dorr continue on to Las Vegas. He needed hospital help. Dorr took the engineer, who was in bad shape by now, to a hospital in Las Vegas and left him. All of this gave much time for Dorr's imagination to create many various possibilities of what might happen now that two strangers to him knew the secret location of the entrance to the river below.

His conclusion was that they would go to Pete Ressler and tell him what had transpired and about the gold that they saw fall from Morton's pocket. So, for that reason he decided to double back, bought some dynamite and hurriedly returned to the caverns. He climbed into the passageway, found the two narrowest locations, lit the fuses, left the cavern, and closed off the entrance to the lost river and the gold below. Dorr figured that this would give him the time he needed to find another entrance down into the caverns, because when he and Morton were in the cave, they had seen a light and felt fresh air coming from one of the side caverns, which indicated another possible entrance.

After giving time for the fumes to clear, Dorr reentered the passageway to see what the results were of his attempt to hide the way to the river. To his surprise, even he could not find the way that they had gone. Satisfied, he decided it was time to return to Nipton and spend some time with Pearl. He briefly stopped to visit with Dave on his way through Cima. The meeting of Slim and Shorty never was brought up other than Dave asking if he had seen them and Dorr saying he had not and had no idea who he was talking about.

As Dorr left Cima to continue on to Nipton, fear began to enter his imagination. What if they hadn't gone to Pete Ressler's but had, instead, gotten equipment and entered the cave for the gold for themselves? What if they were on the river side of the blast when he set off the dynamite, sealing them in the cave? It would only take time to answer. But, how much time? What would the answer be?

CHAPTER **38**

AS EARL ENTERED Nipton he could sense something might have changed since leaving about a week ago. As he passed "The Shaft" and the "Gold Dust" it seemed a little quieter than usual but he could hear the music from the hotel farther down the street.

"Well. Welcome back to town, Earl."

Earl turned to see the sheriff approaching from behind.

"Howdy, Jeff. How has everything been this past week?"

"All pretty quiet," the sheriff replied. "Pearl only had one problem but she handled it just fine."

"Does not surprise me," Earl replied. "You know her background by now, I am sure."

"Yes," the sheriff replied. "But, I do not see a bad person there. She had to do what she had to do to survive. That is all. You are a good man for what you have done for her. Giving her a chance like you have."

"What did she do while I was gone, Jeff?" Earl inquired.

"Oh, nothing. Just shot someone's balls off. He deserved it."

"Oh, shit," Earl replied trying, but failing to hold in his laughter. "Was it Pearl he bothered?"

"No. It was Emit Johnson. He beat up on her girl, Judy."

"Well. Good for her. Protecting her girls," Earl complimented her.

"I guess the doc saved a ball and put a bunch of stitches in his cock. It will be a long time before he bothers any girl again," Jeff commented.

"I think I will go to the "Gold Dust" for a drink," Earl announced. "Join me?"

"Sure," Jeff replied. "Time I looked around down there anyway."

"Hi, Tim," the sheriff announced their arrival as they entered the "Gold Dust" and walked up to the man standing back to them in back of the bar counter. "How are you doing?"

"What the Hell is he doing in here?" Tim responded as he madly pointed his shaking finger at Earl."

"Look what that crazy bitch of his did to Emit," directing his attention to the man sitting on two pillows at a corner table with a bottle and obviously self-medicating.

"Oh. Him," Earl responded as he looked in the direction of the man with what appeared to be a supply of ice at his disposal.

"Need some more ice?" Earl offered.

"Fuck you," was his only reply.

"Come on, Tim," Earl said as he turned towards him.

"You know Pearl was protecting her girls. That man deserved what he got." Earl tried to move the conversation away from the suffering of the pillow man. "How about a drink and talk a little business" Earl suggested.

"Ya. What harm can it do?" the owner Tim replied. "Join us sheriff?"

"Sure. I would like to hear what you guys can work out. Send another bottle over to Johnson," Jeff suggested. "Possibly he has learned something. If not. At least he is being quiet."

"Bob. Go over to "The Shaft" and get Larry to join us," Tim ordered.

"Ya, Boss," he obliged as he walked out the door on his way to the saloon a couple doors down the street.

It was no more than ten minutes and Larry had joined the boys at the table.

"What are we sitting here for?" were the first words out of Larry's mouth.

"To try and find a place for all of us," Earl responded. "Pearl is a tough girl. Four years in Yuma Territorial Prison taught her how to fight. She did what she had to do to survive. She will do what she has to here also to survive. There have been no problems unless some asshole goes up there and starts something. What has Pearl done?" Earl asked.

Receiving no response Earl continued. "You guys have your customers. Pearl has hers. She may have taken some from you. They came from somewhere. Must have been you. But, she did not go for them. They came to her. It is up to you to get them back."

"I agree with all he is saying," Sheriff Jeff spoke up. "Keep these assholes here or tell them to behave up there at the hotel." Suddenly a gunshot fired shattering the bottle of whiskey on the table.

"I will beat the brains out of her for this," Johnson yelled from the corner table as he sat nursing his dick and one ball.

As the boys at the table regrouped and shook off the pieces of glass, they paused in silence.

"Bob," Tim called his right hand man one more time. "Go to the livery and get that Emit Johnson's horse and bring it around front."

"Saddle or no saddle?"

"Saddle," Earl responded. "I want the ride to last a while," bringing a laugh from all. By now Emit had passed out and did not notice the men approaching.

"What the Hell you doing?" Johnson stuttered as he became aware of something happening. He was soon to find out as the men dragged him out to his horse holding his crotch with ice in place.

"You are not putting me on that horse," the man pleaded.

"Put one pillow up there," Sheriff Jeff instructed. "Let's be generous."

They were not exactly gentle as they placed the groaning Johnson on his horse.

"Slap his ass," Earl told anyone near the horse. "Let's hear him yell. Oh. And direct him past the hotel."

"Wait. I will go tell Pearl to come outside," Bob offered. After a few minutes Bob spotted Pearl talking with her show girls.

"Pearl, would you please come outside on the boardwalk," Bob requested as he got her attention. As soon as she recognized who he was, she gave him her complete attention.

"Do you really think it is smart for you to come here?" Pearl asked with shock and anger in her tone.

"Earl is back. He is outside and said he has a surprise for you," he replied.

"He better be there," Pearl warned. "If he is not you will wish you were that sorry shithead Emit Johnson."

Without hesitation, Pearl led the way to the front of the hotel. "Well?"

Suddenly she heard the "ass slap" of a horse followed by the agonizing yells of a man in great pain. As the horse ran by she saw who it was and yelled pleasure in words no one could understand followed by laughter that brought tears to her eyes. For several minutes the yelling continued but was becoming quite weak as the distance increased from which the horse was taking his rider.

"He is going to have a bad day," Pearl commented as she began to walk towards the "Gold Dust" where Earl and the others were standing laughing, patting each other on the back.

"Never would I have believed this," Jeff commented. "All of you out here laughing together."

"May never again, either," Tim warned. "Though if it can happen once I guess it could again."

By then Pearl and Earl had found each other and were lip locked.

"O. K., back to business," Larry said. "But, it has been fun."

"Welcome back," the sheriff said as he parted and walked towards his office.

With a wave of their hands, lips still locked, Pearl and Earl walked to the hotel and straight up the stairs to their room.

"I sure am glad to have you back here," Pearl started as they entered the room. "I was so worried that something would go wrong and that I would never see you again."

"All went fine," Earl assured her.

"Did you find the river?" Pearl inquired.

"Yes. The river is there," Earl answered.

"I had to blast it shut until I can make further plans as to what to do now that it is known by others and it is on another claim," Earl added. "But I will figure out something."

He purposely never mentioned the possible problem with Slim and Shorty and the increasing possibility that they were accidentally on the inside when he blasted the passageway shut.

"Enough," Pearl interrupted. "Let's make up for lost time and pull the bed sheets back."

"That sounds like an offer I am not going to refuse," Earl agreed as he sat in the chair next to the bed and quickly pulled his boots off.

CHAPTER 39

MUCH TIME WAS to pass before any more activity could continue on Kokoweef Mountain. It was confirmed that Dorr had not given the correct information when submitting for the claim. That the cavern entrance was, in fact, on property owned by Pete Ressler.

Despite the fact the county sheriff could prove nothing in the disappearance of the two men, and the entire case lay dormant, suspicions still remained as to what happened and as to what part Dorr actually had in the mystery. But, for this reason, Pete Ressler held Dorr in ill-repute for having trespassed and set off dynamite on his property, and would not agree to allow him to work on his property thereby eliminating access to the cavern. Seven years elapsed before the statute of limitations passed and freed Dorr from any possible guilt in the disappearance of Slim and Shorty.

During the seven years, Earl and Pearl continued to operate the Nipton Hotel very successfully, allowing Earl time and funds to accumulate equipment and begin his continuing search for another entrance to the caverns below that would lead to the river. Dorr also had sent John Herman, a Pasadena, California, assayer, a 2 ½ pound sample of the black sands, and his report showed $2,145.47 a cubic yard with gold at $20.47 an ounce. He also had determined through engineering measurements and observations that it would take a three hundred fifty foot tunnel to penetrate the caverns at a point one thousand feet below the present entrance.

Earl had formed a friendship and interest in his exploration with two men, Herman Wallace and Stephen Kelly. Together they formed a company and acquired additional sophisticated equipment and continued explorations at Kokoweef Cave in the east side of the mountain, at a fault line which Dorr believed bisected Crystal Cave within the mountain.

Soon the Depression days of 1932-1941 arrived and all work at Kokoweef was suspended. Also, at this time, Pete Ressler, now old and quite ill, had made an agreement with Stephen Kelly, the only man he trusted, that would allow digging in Crystal Cave which was on his property and within the original passageway. Dorr had no choice now but to follow along with the association as low man on the totem pole. Hard feelings began to develop between Dorr and Kelly that would last a lifetime.

Work was begun on the mountain in earnest, but before excavations proceded much beyond Kokoweef Caverns, a vein of carbonate zinc was located. Much to the dismay of Dorr, work on searching for the river stopped, and the Carbonate King Zinc Mine went into full operation on the south side of the mountain.

Dorr warned that the blasting may close forever the passageway he and Morton had used to reach the river. His warnings went unheeded because of the million dollars' worth of zinc being found and the subsidizing of the Carbonate King Mine, by the government.

Due to the hard feelings that had developed between Steven Kelly and Dorr, Kelly joined Klaus Russ and Herman Wallace and formed Kokoweef Associates which later became Crystal Cave Mining Corporation of Nevada. By way of a patented claim, they became sole owners of the Kokoweef complex network of caverns and tunnels and left Earl Dorr out completely.

Dorr left the group very angry and filed his own claim nine miles away in the Mescale Mountains in a natural cave that he hoped would lead to a second entrance. Times had been hard on Dorr ever since he blasted shut the first entrance with the unproven possibility that it led to the death of two men. He struck out on his own which led to no success.

In the meantime, Pearl continued to run the Nipton Hotel as

best she could. That too was running out its course. Time was hard on Nipton as most of the gold mines had closed and the zinc mines were closing as the vein in the Carbonate King mine had played out. The population had reduced and Pearl's shows, including her stagecoach robbery, were no longer a draw. Her girls had aged and the brothel near closed. The time had come to move on and complete the journey she had started so long ago. To return to Globe, Arizona.

It had been eight years now and it appeared as if Earl had disappeared into the desert looking for that other entrance to the underground river. The depression had hit even the mining community. The hotel had become nearly empty.

"Good morning, Pearl," the sheriff greeted Pearl as he and James arrived for their usual breakfast. "How are you this morning?"

"I am O.K.," Pearl replied. "The usual this morning, boys?"

"Yes, please," James answered.

"I meant to ask," Pearl added, "Whatever happened to Earl? After he blasted the entrance to the underground river, he went off looking for another way to the caverns. I have never seen or heard from him since that day. It has been many years. He must have had an accident. I just can't seem to find a way to close it out of my mind."

"I am sure that you are right," the sheriff answered. "We searched everywhere. We had nothing else that we could do. You know that. He told no one where he was going."

"I know. It is sad," Pearl agreed. "But, I must go on. I will not be here much longer."

Pearl left the men at the table and walked into the kitchen area.

"Sure is not the way it used to be around here," the sheriff commented. "Never thought the day would come when Pearl would be cooking breakfast for us instead of eating with us."

"I know," James agreed. "Pearl said that if the right person came along, she would be gone in a minute." Pearl returned with their breakfast.

"Why don't you join us?" James offered.

"I would but I have another customer."

"Oh, I didn't see him," James responded as he turned to look around the dining room, seeing a man sitting by himself.

"Excuse me," Pearl said as she turned and walked over to the other man's table.

"Any idea who he is?" James asked looking at the sheriff. "I have seen him around a couple of times. He comes into the store, buys a few things, then leaves without a hint of who he is or what he is doing in the area."

"I have no idea," the sheriff answered. "I have not met him. But, I understand that he is the Front Engineer for a mining company. He has been looking at the Carbonate King as a possible source of zinc. I guess he is hired to locate mining possibilities, and then moves on."

"That could be a good sign for Nipton," James commented.

"It could be, but not likely. I think I will go over and introduce myself while Pearl is in the kitchen," the sheriff said as he stood up and walked towards the other man's table.

"I have seen you around lately. Just thought I would come over and introduce myself. I am Sheriff Beckett. Just call me Sheriff."

"Nice to meet you, my name is Cal Bywater."

"May I ask what might your business be, sir?"

"Just land transfer. I am helping Pete Ressler sell a few claims to the Crystal Cave Mining Company."

"Have you closed the deal yet?"

"Yes," Cal replied. "But, I will be around for a few days at least. Need to talk to Pearl some more. I want to purchase some land in Arizona. Maybe I will work a small copper claim and raise a few cattle. I am sick of the travel."

The sheriff tipped his hat and returned to his table as he noticed Pearl delivering their breakfast.

"Something is in the air that we know nothing about," the sheriff told James as he returned and sat at the table.

"What are you talking about?" James questioned.

"He says that he is done around here, but will be staying a few days to talk to Pearl. Not only that, he wants to go to Arizona. You know who else wants to go there."

James said nothing, but did look in the direction of the man's table as he saw Pearl heading that way with his meal. He watched as Pearl placed his breakfast on the table then sat down to talk with him.

"Well, that is out of character for Pearl," James commented.

"I am going to stay in town tonight," Cal informed Pearl. "I am sure you have a room."

"Oh ya, I have plenty of rooms."

"Would you join me for dinner tonight?" Cal offered.

"I would love to, Cal," Pearl agreed.

"That is wonderful. I must be out of town until early evening. Will that be alright?"

"I will have someone covering tonight so we can enjoy the evening," Pearl answered.

"Great, I will be back as early as I can," Cal promised.

Cal left for the day to finish up the Crystal Cave Mining Company deal that would free him from any further obligation.

"What have you got going?" James quizzed Pearl as he passed her on his way out of the room.

Pearl did not reply except for a gleam in her eye no one had seen from her for a very long time. Evening arrived finding Pearl in the saloon part of the hotel with a couple of the girls enjoying a couple of drinks. They all knew that Pearl would be leaving soon. What they did not know was what her plans were for the hotel. What would they do when Pearl did leave? Sheriff Beckett entered the saloon and sat at a far table. Pearl saw him and walked over to join him. As soon as she sat down Cal entered and walked to the table where they were sitting.

"Good evening, Pearl, Sheriff," Cal greeted them.

"Good evening Cal," the Sheriff acknowledged. "You made it back, have a seat. Would you like a whiskey?"

"Yes, thank you. And how are you Sheriff?"

"I was just telling the Sheriff how I have been thinking that I might turn this place over to the girls and finish my journey to Globe. Nothing is holding me here anymore," Pearl caught Cal up on the conversation.

"That would be a good area for your ranch, Cal," the Sheriff suggested. "It would be much better than this area."

"I am now done around here," Cal said. "I just might go up there and check it out."

"May I go with you?" Pearl asked to the surprise of all including Cal.

"Only if it means that you would be my girl," Cal responded.

"If that is what it takes," Pearl replied. "Are you married?"

"No," was Cal's one word answer.

"Sounds like you two have some important things to talk about. It is time for me to check out the street anyway." The Sheriff rose from the table, tipped his hat, and left the room.

"You know," Pearl spoke up as she looked Cal straight in the eye, "considering all that you have heard, I have nothing against Earl. We rode into this town together. We didn't know each other at the time. I had to stay here a couple of days before my connection to Globe arrived where I had intended to go. He had taken good care of me for the first few years. He made it possible for me to have this hotel. That is why I stayed here. We did develop a strong relationship but that is all. We never married. I have stayed loyal to him. But he has been gone eight years. There is no relationship anymore. His mind is out there, if he is alive, in the desert somewhere. I don't even think that he remembers who he truly is anymore. The desert has a way of doing that to a person after a while."

"I am sorry about that Pearl," Cal replied. "But, I am serious. In a day or two I am going to head out and go to Globe to see what is up there. I am sick of traveling. There must be something up there. I know that I am getting too old for hard rock mining, but, a war is in the future. You can just feel it. That would make the price of copper high enough to live off. There are small stakes that I could work and get a few cattle. You could help me get it up and running. We both have had enough that we could be self-sufficient and happy that way."

"I am serious also," Pearl interjected. "I know the area well. I know where there are likely to be abandoned claim sites. I think we could do it together and live out our lives in peace."

Cal was an attractive, pleasant man. He was about five feet nine inches, weighed 180 pounds, light hair and blue eyes. Very attractive to Pearl. It had become obvious to all.

"Would you like to shake on a deal?" Cal offered.

"I know a better way to sign a deal," Pearl suggested. "Follow me to me to my room. You will make me happy and it will be a deal."

"I like the way you do business. Shall we seal the deal now?" Cal suggested.

"Well, I am ready," Pearl agreed as she rose from the table.

"Then let's go sign the deal," Cal complied.

Pearl was surprised the following morning to find that Cal had already left. Lying in the bed, staring at the ceiling in silence, brought her to the realization that Nipton was actually holding her prisoner. For the past few years as Earl slipped out of her life, she had been blind to the truth that the world had fallen into shattered pieces of a past dream which she was only trying to hold on to as the pieces kept becoming more scattered and much smaller. She gradually brought herself back to reality, dressed, and walked down to the hotel lobby.

"Good morning Pearl," Jesse greeted her. "You certainly seem to have a glow about you this morning."

"You just pay no attention to my glow. Where is Cal?"

"He left much earlier. He said that he had one paper for the Wallace family to sign and that he would be right back soon," Jesse informed Pearl. "He seems like a real nice person, Pearl."

"Yes," Pearl agreed. "That is what scares me. Maybe he is too nice."

"He said to tell you that he would be ready to leave in two days and that you would know what he means."

"I need to talk to the girls," Pearl said. "Would you please ask them to be here at noon and that it is very important."

"Of course," Jesse obliged. "I will have them all here waiting for you."

"I will be back shortly," Pearl assured Jesse. "I am going over to see James and Linda."

"Yes Pearl."

Pearl Left and walked slowly to the mercantile looking at every building on the way as if to seal the picture in her mind.

"Good morning Pearl," Linda greeted Pearl.

"Good morning, Linda, Jim," Pearl greeted them in return. "I came here just to let you know that I will be leaving Nipton within a couple of days."

"Oh no" Linda spoke up in sadness. "I had heard something was about to change. We hate to see you leave. You have become such a part of our family and town over the years. It just could never be the same without you here."

"I know and thank you," Pearl softly acknowledged. "But, the town is not what I want anymore. I am tired of running the hotel. I am not happy now that Earl is but a figment of my memory. He will always be a good man in my memory. But, he is not in my life anymore and it is time I moved on. It is obvious by now that he never again will be in my life. I am lonely and I want to move on to Globe where I want to end my life's journey that I started so many years ago. I have a chance to go now with Cal. I must not lose the opportunity."

"Do you know what you will do there?" James asked.

"Not for sure but we will start a life together and will be happy." Pearl assured him.

"The girls are waiting for you in the saloon," Jesse informed Pearl as he poked his head into the mercantile.

"I am leaving the hotel for you and Linda to run as your own," Pearl started to explain to James. "It will be yours to have and run until the day Earl returns if he ever does. I will have a paper drawn up that we can sign this afternoon that in case of his death or certificate of the fact, the hotel will be yours to own. I am taking the original $10,000 that was invested. The rest is yours. There will be a balance sheet available this afternoon also. I am going to talk to the girls now and explain everything. I know that they all will stay, and Jesse also, and that it will be status quo when you take over."

Pearl then left to return to the saloon to have a conversation with the girls.

"Pour me a double whiskey, Jesse," Pearl requested as soon as she entered the saloon.

"I hear rumors Pearl," Judy, one of the girls spoke up. "Are the rumors true?"

"If it is that I am leaving the hotel and the town, then, yes it is true." Pearl answered. "The town has slowed down too much for me. I have an opportunity to leave with Cal and go to Globe and that is what I want to do. James and Linda will be taking over the hotel. Everyone here, including you Jesse, will stay on and keep your same job as it is now with me."

The goodbyes were short. The hugs were long. The tears were many. Just as Pearl was going to leave the saloon Cal walked in. Pearl walked to him and gave him a big hug.

"Cal," Pearl backs away and looks at him. "Aren't you ready to leave town?"

"Well, I am now."

"Then if you are ready why don't you get your stuff and let's get the hell out of here," Pearl requested. "All of my stuff is packed and ready and I am ready. Why wait another day?"

"O.K., I will not unhitch the horses," Cal responded. "Let's load up and go. The weather is fine. Even when dark sets in the moon is full. It can guide us down the road."

"I have done it without the moon," Pearl spoke up.

"When was that?"

"Never mind," Pearl answered.

The Sheriff arrived and saw the action.

"Going someplace?"

"Yes, we are leaving now," Pearl answered. "It is time to go. We are all loaded and ready. It is too hard to sit around and look at each other."

"Let's have a couple drinks together before we hit the road," Pearl requested.

Jesse brought the whiskey to the table, opened it and poured the first round.

"Come on Jesse, sit and join us," Pearl offered.

After a few rounds it was decided that the time had arrived to leave.

"Come on Pearl," Cal reached for her hand. "The wagon is ready so let's load up and head for Searchlight.""

"Here are some food and drink for you two," Linda said as she set them in the back of the wagon. As they waved and blew kisses, Cal swished the reins and the horses responded by pulling the buck wagon away from the hotel and out of Nipton as all parties finished their last goodbyes.

"We are on our way. On our way to start our new life together," Cal said as they were about to lose sight of Nipton now far in the distance.

"I am happy," Pearl spoke up. "But, it really isn't the way I wanted it to end in Nipton. It was real nice for several years. The romantic part of the search for the river and the caverns, and the assay report being so positive was exciting. But, I sure am happy you came along."

"If Earl never finds that underground river with all that gold, if it is there, someone will find it sometime," Cal said of his belief. "People will come and go looking until it is found or proven not to be there."

"Let's move ahead and beyond the past," Cal suggested. "Let's grab the air as it flows by us and let it pull us away from the past and into the future life that we are now starting together."

Pearl snuggled up to Cal, put her head in his lap and silently but for the sound of the wagon, they travel on towards their first destination, Searchlight, Nevada. When they reached Searchlight Pearl could not believe her eyes. When she was last in Searchlight, about ten years ago, the town was declining. The hotels were closed where she purchased the furnishings for their hotel, but there must have been nearly 1000 people living there. Now it appeared to be less than 100. The mines had closed when she was here last but the Arrowhead High, the new road to Los Angeles, kept the town alive. Now another highway had been built that bypassed Searchlight altogether.

"This town is in worse shape than Nipton," Pearl commented. "Everything is gone. There is one hotel, the Colten. We can stay there."

"Sounds fine to me," Cal agreed. Cal parked the wagon in front of the hotel and they walked in and approached the desk clerk.

"We would like a room, please," Cal requested.

"I have two rooms. One with a bath and one with a common bath for the floor," the desk clerk offered.

"That is all you have? I am surprised. The town looks dead," Cal commented.

"We would be, but, we have many long term tenants," the desk clerk explained. "They work on the new Hoover Dam."

"Oh. I will need the room with a bath," Cal requested. "Would there be a bus to Needles? We need to catch a train there."

"Sure, there is one that arrives at 9 in the morning," he informed Cal. "What about the wagon and horses?"

"One hundred dollars and it is yours," Cal offered.

"You've got a deal and I will throw the room in for free," the desk clerk agreed and handed Cal five twenty dollar bills.

"Thank you very much. We will be retiring to our room now. Big day tomorrow," Cal replied.

"Good night, sir."

In the morning Cal and Pearl boarded the waiting bus for the next part of Pearl's journey to Globe. The bus pulled away from the hotel and slowly disappeared on the one road south to Needles. It was evening when the bus arrived in Needles.

"Does this train take us all the way to Globe?" Pearl Inquired.

"No. We will have to switch in Phoenix," Cal informed her.

"I really would like to go back to Dripping Springs," Pearl requested. "I know the area and I think there is an abandoned claim there that we could work together. I knew somebody who had a claim there and later went to prison. We lived there for a while. It is near the Old Dominion Mine. Last I knew the guy went to Mexico. No one would care if we work it unless someone is there."

"We will check it out," Cal offered. It is only a few miles from Globe. The first thing we will do when we get to Globe is buy a truck."

It took three days but the travelers finally arrived in Globe, Arizona.

"I never did quite get to Globe when I lived in the area," Pearl offered. "It is much bigger than I thought."

"I will find a truck that we can buy. Why don't you go to the mercantile and pick out what we will need," Cal suggested.

As soon as they had the truck loaded they headed out of town and into the hills that surrounded Globe. After about an hour the well maintained dirt road Pearl directed Cal to take turned into a very rough, unmaintained dirt road that led them into a narrow gorge.

"You are sure about where we are going aren't you?" Cal asked cautiously.

Pearl didn't answer, but pointed her hand straight ahead. After about three miles they came upon a very dilapidated shack and two small outhouses.

"This is it," Pearl exclaimed with excitement as if it were a castle. "It sure looks a lot worse than when I was here before. But, that was 37 years ago. Doesn't look like any one has been here since," Pearl suggested.

"So, there is gold here?" Cal questioned.

"No. There was silver and that ran out, so they mined copper," Pearl answered.

"The copper was worth very little then," Cal commented. "But, it is not any more. We may be able to mine enough to live on. At least there is a roof. I can go to Globe and get what I need to make it livable after we check everything out. Where is the big mine you told me about? There must be water there."

"The big mine is about a half mile farther up the road," Pearl informed Cal. "But, there is a spring only about fifty yards from here and a wash that flows in the winter when it rains. But the spring always was dripping and flowing down a small rock out-cropping. It is where this spot got its name, Dripping Springs. It was like a small town then. When you have time you will find more buildings up the road."

Cal did walk to the spring and found that it was as Pearl explained. He also could see that with a little work he could re-direct the water to pass very close to the shack. He then walked up the road and found what was left of the town. There was a collection of crude wooden structures scattered among the mine tailings and dumps. There also was evidence of several that were destroyed by fire.

Meanwhile Pearl had cleaned up the shack and organized what she could. It was at least livable for the meantime. Pearl had, after 42 years, completed her journey. The peace and safety she had looked for she had found.

Pearl had managed to keep her true identity and history a secret. Pearl and Cal were married on their first return visit to Globe, and Pearl Bywater would be the name she would use in her later years. There came a day, when Cal was in Globe, when a woman pretending to be a census taker in 1940 visited their location. She noticed that Pearl was shabbily dressed and that the cabin was quite the sight. It was obvious that Cal and Pearl were barely living off the land. Through a series of questions, the mystery of the "Bandit Queen" was revealed. The woman was Clara Wooly, a newspaper writer, who was taking the census. She saw no reason to expose Pearl's secret and protected her secret until Pearl's death.

The following years were very uneventful. Cal and Pearl lived a peaceful life keeping to themselves. They did manage to recover enough silver and copper to purchase a few head of cattle and became self-sufficient.

In 1950 Cal suffered a massive heart attack which totally disabled him to a degree that required Pearl to place him in a facility in Globe. Pearl continued to live by herself in the cabin by the spring that she shared with Cal. She did fulfill her promise she had made to herself when leaving private school at the age of seventeen to escape its stringent controls and her abusive father. That promise was to be able to do what she wanted, go where she wanted, and most importantly, be free.

George Calvin Bywater died on August 17th, 1955, of coronary occlusion. Pearl did move shortly after Cal died to Globe and lived at 156 E. Mesquite Street. Pearl Taylor Hart Bywater, who had become, and should still be remembered as, "a voice for women's freedom and liberation," died four months and eleven days after Cal on December 28th, 1955, of uremia and cardiovascular disease at the age of 84.

George Calvin Bywater and Pearl Taylor Bywater are resting in peace together in the Pinal Cemetery, located between Globe and Claypool, Arizona.

Pearl and Cal's Gravestone

Pearl Hart

Pearl Hart.

Mug Shot of Pearl Hart upon Entrance to
Yuma Territorial Prison, Yuma, AZ

Pearl Reading a Letter in Yuma Territorial Prison

Author's Personal Photographs
of Kokoweef Mine

Climbing down Jacob's Ladder

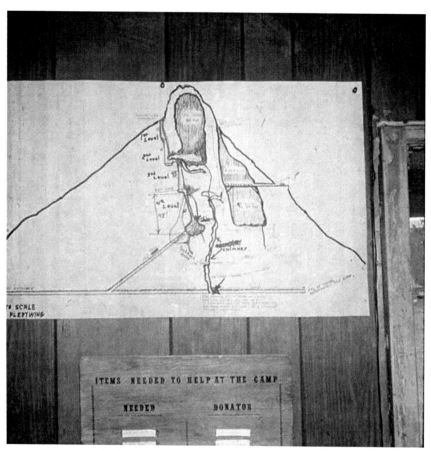

Drawing Made in 1974 Showing Work Done by the Author's Crew

Author in Foreground in Sky Room

Inside Crystal Room Looking up at Crossing Bridge

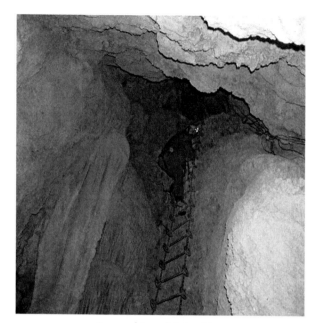

Second Jacob's Ladder

Readying Second Ladder below Jacob's Ladder #2 into Schnar's Hole

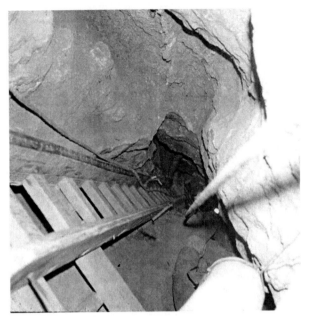

Looking into Schnar's Hole

Climbing down Wooden Ladder into Schnar's Hole

Entrance to Sky Room

Author inside Sky Room

Climbing down Jacob's Ladder #2

View of the Climb down

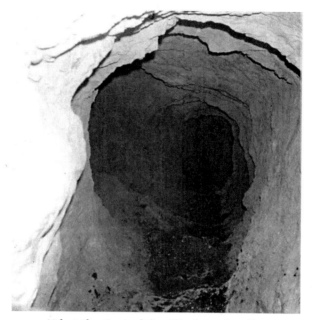

What the Rest of the Climb Looks Like

Author's Father Looking into Natural Opening